Rebecca has the pen of a poet and the heart of a disciple—which makes At Home in My Heart *stirring and relevant.*

PATSY CLAIRMONT
Author of *It's about Home* and
Stardust on My Pillow

[This is] a beautiful and simple how-to instruction book for the heart and home. As you step inside Rebecca's door on this very unrestricted tour, you are made aware of the changes that [may] need to be made in your own heart and home.

Renovation began in my heart early into the tour. Definitely inspired and timed by the Master Designer. Without a doubt written for me.

GLYNDA TURLEY
Renowned Artist and Illustrator

At Home in My Heart *gives you the tools you need for Heart Improvement. Its pages will inspire you to renovate, restore, and redecorate from the inside out.*

FLORENCE LITTAUER
Author of *Personality Plus* and *Silver Boxes*

An artist with words, Rebecca Barlow Jordan uses humor and stories as she shares her journey to the heart of God. I could not wait to get to the next chapter, knowing I would be challenged in my walk with God.

Women will love and reread this book.

ESTHER BURROUGHS
Speaker and Author of *Empowered*
and *Splash the Living Water*

The words of this book simply but effectively show how to make your heart a beautiful refuge—a warm, inviting place where love dwells and peace reigns.

EMILIE BARNES
Lecturer and Author

I'm intrigued by secrets. I'm improved when I search my heart. I'm encouraged by loving touches.

When Rebecca packages these three together in this book, we can get a stimulating, challenging, and delightful basket of goodies for daily living. She takes her everyday experiences and weaves them into our hearts, moving us to want more of the presence of God. She reminds me that, "Home is truly where the heart is."

THELMA WELLS,
Speaker and Author
A Woman of God Ministries, Dallas, Texas

Women love open houses and model homes. We like to see what others have done within their four walls. In At Home in My Heart—Preparing a Place for His Presence, *Rebecca Barlow Jordan takes our inherent interest in real estate and focuses it on the Real Estate—the heart of Christ. Each chapter is like a session of "This Old House," helping us remodel, rebuild, and restore the rooms in our hearts.*

MARITA LITTAUER
President, CLASServices Inc.,
Speaker/Author of
Come As You Are, Love Extravagantly

With her tender, poignant pen, Rebecca writes to the soul of any woman who's yearned for a makeover of home and heart. Filled with images of gardens, quiet mountain moments, and homey nooks, this talented writer touches upon the visual scenes women love and applies their lessons to the blossoming of our individual hearts.

BECKY FREEMAN
Author and Speaker

At Home in My Heart *is a book for every woman who longs to be transformed into a person who reflects simple elegance, renewed joy, appropriate strength, grace under pressure, abundant mercy, and authentic spirituality. With heart-grabbing quotations, true stories, practical how-tos, biblical counsel, probing questions, and follow-through application, Rebecca Barlow Jordan has written a book that will help you to redecorate your heart—from the inside out!*

CAROL KENT
President, Speak Up Speaker Services,
Author of *Becoming a Woman of Influence*

At Home in My Heart

PREPARING A PLACE
FOR HIS PRESENCE

REBECCA BARLOW JORDAN

PROMISE
PRESS
An Imprint of Barbour Publishing

Published by Promise Press, an imprint of Barbour Publishing, Inc., P.O. Box 719, Uhrichsville, Ohio 44683, www.promisepress.com

Member of the
Evangelical Christian
Publishers Association

Printed in the United States of America.

Dedication

With gratitude
To the Loves of My Life—
Larry, Valerie, and Jennifer,
Who have made our house
A true home and haven on earth—
And to the Lover of My Soul
Who patiently and willingly
Makes Himself
At home in my heart.

Contents

Special Thanks

Writing a book like this is like building a house. The home-owner has a dream house in mind, but it takes many experts and their loving skills to make that home a reality. This house would have never passed the building inspection had it not been for the fantastic contributions of some precious, gifted people.

- Thanks to the editorial, sales, and marketing staff at Promise Press who liked the blueprints, believed in my dream, and contributed hands-on labor in the final building stages.

- To my friend, Barbara Sims, who introduced me to Promise Press.

- To Larry, my husband, soul mate, and best friend, who served as my unofficial building inspector and eliminated any unnecessary room additions. For your unswerving integrity, the endless hours you spent editing, and the bowls of soup you endured (and sometimes cooked) while I hammered away, and for your faithful love, prayers, encouragement, and belief in my dream and my abilities—how can I thank you enough? I love you!

- To my daughters, Valerie and Jennifer, and their hus-bands, Shawn and Craig, for their encouragement, love, and support throughout the building process. You've made this house a home! Thanks to you and to other family members, Bob, Tricia, and Mom, who allowed me to add their names and stories to the rooms of my heart. I love all of you!

- To my support team of women who agreed to hold me accountable and furnished my house with prayers throughout the entire process: Ruth Inman, Priscilla Adams, Sharon Hogan, and Mary Griffin. Thanks for your valuable insight. You're wonderful!

- To my fellow writing friends, "The Hens with Pens": Becky Freeman, Suzie Duke, Gracie Malone, and Fran Sandin, who have encouraged my dream house from its inception. Thanks, Suzie, for painting the final title on the house.

- Thanks to friends, Karen, Millie, and Chet, loving members of our church, Attagirls, and endless others for your prayerful support.

- Thanks most of all to my precious Architect—the Lord Jesus Himself—for allowing this dream house to be a reality—and for filling its rooms with His Presence.

REBECCA BARLOW JORDAN

Introduction

For years I struggled with restlessness in my spirit. I wasn't sure what I wanted, so I began to knock on God's door a little louder. Popular authors cried, "You need simplicity!" so my heart yearned to experience that downsizing—that elimination of cluttered lifestyle. When my husband's new job moved us to a smaller, rural-like atmosphere away from the large city metroplex, I thought, *This is my answer. We'll downsize and maybe even find a cute Victorian cottage in the country where I can decorate to my heart's content.*

We did downsize, but not in the country and not in a Rockwell-style home with wraparound porches. Nevertheless, I set to work plotting out my new decor, one I thought the Lord and I would really like. But in the middle of my decorating frenzy, there was a knock at my door.

"That isn't what you need," I heard from the bold visitor standing on my front porch.

His words pierced my spirit like arrows. This good friend of mine was now acting like a guest—outside my door. "I know the source of your restlessness. It's in your heart. That's where you need a renovation. Let me redesign and simplify your heart. I'll walk with you through your home and remind you again of what's really important. When I'm finished, this will be not a house, but a beautiful home where My presence will abide with you daily."

His gentle voice rang with such authority that I immediately abandoned my remaining plans and invited Him in. His method? Like the psalmist recounting God's goodness throughout the journeys of Israel, He uncovered the "stories" of my heart, pointing out the lessons He had taught me and reminding me of His track record of faithfulness. Gently but firmly, this friend nudged me to remember and renew— always emphasizing the underlying thread of His intentions: to make my heart like His—a place where we both could feel at home daily.

The results of that renovation left me eager to share, just like the Samaritan woman at the well: "Come, see a man who told me everything I ever did."

I did not write this book in a few weeks or a few months. For me, it is the story of a simple, lifelong quest to know the Father and to make my heart a true home for the presence of Jesus. This book is not about me. If all you learn after you turn the last page is what my home and heart look like, in a physical sense, then I have failed. My desire is that you would come to see Jesus.

Perhaps your heart, too, longs for change: renewed joy, simple attitudes, lasting peace. But you're unskilled in this area of redecorating. What if you invited the Master Designer to renovate your heart also? What if He showed you simply but effectively how to make your heart a beautiful refuge—a warm, inviting place where love dwells and peace reigns? He has no fee—except the price of obedience.

May I invite you to join me as we take that journey together? Would you step through the door of my heart and home and meet the One who will also "tell you all you have ever done"?

My heart is still under construction. The Master Designer is always at work redecorating, moving the furniture, and repapering the walls. As a fellow struggler, my heart's desire for you is:

> *That Christ will be more and more at home in your hearts, living within you as you trust in him. May your roots go down deep into the soil of God's marvelous love; and may you be able to feel and understand, as all God's children should, how long, how wide, how deep, and how high his love really is; and to experience this love for yourselves, though it is so great that you will never see the end of it or fully know or understand it. And so at last you will be filled up with God himself.*
> EPHESIANS 3:17–19 TLB

Listen. . . . Could that be Him knocking at the door?
REBECCA BARLOW JORDAN

Change My Heart, Lord

I said, "Lord, I want an escape."

   He said, "Child, you need to wait."

I said, "Lord, I want a change."

   He said, "Child, let me rearrange you."

I said, "Lord, I want the country."

   He said, "Child, there are people in the city."

I said, "Lord, I want to make a difference."

   He said, "Child, I need to make you my disciple."

I said, "Lord, I want some answers."

   He said, "Child, I need your obedience."

I said, "Lord, I want to be happy."

   He said, "Child, you need to be content."

I said, "Lord, I want to advance."

   He said, "Child, you need to retreat."

I said, "Lord, I want to travel to new places."

   He said, "Child, you need to find joy in your journey."

I said, "Lord, I want to find peace."

   He said, "Child, you need to find me."

A Welcome Place

*When you open your heart
to a stranger,
you have welcomed
the Savior as well.*

Keep the Welcome Mat Out

Every home has an invisible welcome sign. When someone walks up our sidewalk, they can sense an attitude of hospitality by the time they reach our front door. Though this house does not sport a wraparound porch filled with rockers, one thing is always present: the welcome mat. Often, the kind of mat people see on our porches reflects the personalities of those inside the home.

Most of you are probably visualizing a straw or rubber mat for depositing earthly burdens (mud, leaves, and gum, for example) at the door. But that's not the kind of mat I'm talking about. The outside mat clues us in to something deeper, something more—invisible. Usually we find one of two responses when we knock on someone's door. In one, the first words out of the hostess's mouth are: "Oh, I'm so sorry, excuse the house, please. It's such a mess." Especially if you are making an unannounced visit. The second woman swings open the door and, like a *Southern Living* hostess, drawls, "Y'all come on in. I'm so glad to see *you*!"

I know many women whose welcome signs are always visible—in their hearts, as well as on their front porches. Margaret was such a woman. Several years ago she invited our family as guests for dinner in her home. When Margaret opened her door, the sound of a Spanish guitar greeted us from the corner entertainment center. The pungent smell of onions, garlic, and sweet fiery peppers floated through the air. Real Mexican food—not your ordinary take-out tacos and burritos. Our mouths were watering before we crossed the hallway into the living room.

Margaret and her husband, both schoolteachers, graciously asked about each of us, even our children. Margaret seemed neither nervous nor anxious, but moved about gracefully like a Spanish dancer in slow motion. Festive, colorful dinnerware graced the dining room table, but there was nothing formal about Margaret's attitude. She seated us, not at the table, but in the living room, pointing to the coffee table where loving hands had prepared a delectable appetizer: fresh homemade salsa and warm chips. Her husband took our drink orders, and in a minute, they both returned with iced tea and water.

I expected Margaret to rush back to the kitchen and finish preparing dinner for us. Instead, she removed her shoes, sat on the floor, and scooted up a pillow around the low coffee table. While we nibbled on the pre-dinner goodies, she stayed and visited. I kept thinking, *This scene is familiar to me.* But it wasn't until later that I realized why.

After we had gorged ourselves with peppery chips and nourishing conversation, Margaret delegated her husband to visit a little longer. Then she returned once again to the kitchen.

Immediately, she began to lay out a sumptuous feast, lovingly prepared beforehand. As we moved toward the dining room, I noticed the carefully detailed touches that adorned the table: fresh homemade rolls, flower-shaped butter pats, and a tossed salad with carrot curls and artful veggies. When we finished her gazpacho soup, cheese enchiladas, beans, and Spanish rice, we

> *If you would have guests merry with cheer, be so yourself, or so at least appear.*
>
> BENJAMIN FRANKLIN

all felt like shouting, "Olé!" "Bravo!" Obviously she knew—and enjoyed—her craft. Just when we thought we couldn't stuff another bite into our mouths, Margaret brought out individual plates of luscious strawberry-filled crepes.

We heard no fuss, no apologies, no grumbling for lack of help, but an ability to converse freely. She gave us her total attention. From the moment we arrived until our late night exit, Margaret's heart and hands said, "Welcome, friends! You are my important guests tonight."

Later as I was thinking and maybe envying Margaret's hospitality skills, I knew why that scene at Margaret's home had seemed so familiar. In that season of my life during my thirties, I considered myself a "Mary"—certainly not a "Martha"—primarily because of my falling soufflés, burnt toast, and *Gone with the Wind* housekeeping habits. When I visited others' homes, I often lingered for quiet, meaningful conversation rather than opt for fussy details in the kitchen.

When I entertained, however, "Martha" suddenly emerged

21

like a Hyde from Dr. Jekyll. I reverted to what Sandra Felton might call "The Irrational Messie." I scrubbed every floor until I could see my face in it, scoured the bathrooms until bleach fumes begged for escape through open windows, dug out all my best Safeway china, tied every white cloth napkin with tiny blue ribbons, and placed small calligraphy placards on every shelf and table in the house. By the time company arrived, however, dinner was still steaming in the kitchen—and so was I.

When my guests rang the doorbell, I hastily opened the door, issued a quick hug, and then ran back to my marathon of stirring, mixing, chopping, and simmering. Most of the time, company followed me into the kitchen, where I quickly enlisted them in kitchen duty, or my husband, Larry, kept them entertained in the living room until dinner was ready. By the time I sat down, my body was too tired or numb to even hear the conversation, much less enjoy it.

———

When I invited Jesus into my home as Master Designer, I thought of Margaret. Jesus looked down at my front porch and spoke gently, almost in a whisper: "You need a new welcome mat."

Embarrassed, I glanced down at the frayed piece of straw on my front porch and realized my welcome mat had become fuzzy and worn. Maybe I had even turned it upside down or bleached the words right off in one of my cleaning fits. The word "Welcome" was no longer visible.

I looked at the One who received all His guests—friends

and strangers alike—with open arms, and I knew He had started at the right place. To Jesus, no one was a stranger. Child or leper, thief or priest saw "welcome" on the front door of His heart. He had no roof over His head, no place to call His own. Yet Jesus knew how to create mansions out of tents.

What to serve His guests? Not a problem for Jesus. With a prayer of thanks and a touch of His hands, He transformed even the smallest of offerings into plentiful feasts. He's always ready for good conversation and is more concerned with a clean heart than a clean house.

Jesus is a friend for the friendless, a home for the homeless, and hope for the hopeless.

Gradually, with the Master Designer's help, I am overcoming those old habits. Now, each time I open the door and see my new personalized welcome mat, it reminds me that the people who walk across my threshold are some of the most precious gifts I am privileged to enjoy.

Maybe it's not how big a kitchen I have, how lush a meal I can prepare, or even how beautifully I can set a table. "Welcome" is an attitude written on my heart, everywhere I go. I don't want others to see, "Too busy, come back later." If my life happens to be in disarray at the moment, maybe I can at least say, "Under construction—but come on in, anyway!"

Since living in East Texas, I have been practicing my simple, Southern welcome. When people drop by, no longer am I apologizing, "I'm sorry about my house." Whether it's family, friends, or neighbors, instead the greeting is, "I'm so glad to see *y'all*. Come on in here. Let's visit for awhile."

⌒

Master Designer Secret

*"You're fussing far too much
and getting yourself worked
up over nothing.
One thing only is essential,
and Mary has chosen it—
it's the main course,
and won't be taken from her."*

LUKE 10:41–42 THE MESSAGE

Heart Check

*When others approach
the front door of your heart,
what kind of welcome mat do they see?*

Loving Touches

PERSONALIZED WELCOME MAT

One woven, straw mat (any shape)
2–3 yards of your favorite ribbon, any color
Wood cutout of heart or other shape
Small jars of acrylic paint, any colors

At your local discount or variety store, purchase a woven, straw mat. These braided mats are usually inexpensive and easy to work with. Paint your favorite wood shape any color with your acrylic paints. Let it dry. Then print or stencil your "welcome phrase" or your name. Let it dry. Weave ribbon in and out all around the edges, beginning and ending at the top center of the mat. Tie in a small bow, or glue on a premade ribbon bow at the top center with a hot glue gun. Glue the dried wood shape to the mat, directly under the bow. Instead of a wood cutout, you can use waxed fruit or silk flowers. Be creative. And remember, this is usually the first thing someone sees as they step onto your porch. How would you like to greet those who knock at your door? Here's a thought:

If you like home and simple places,
Come on in and show your faces.

A Master Plan

- Plan two or three simple menus—ones you can easily prepare for company—no matter how large or small the crowd. Keep some frozen meals on hand for emergencies.

- Delegate chores for housecleaning, food preparation, and cleanup.

- Play a tape of soft instrumental or praise music before and during the meal.

- Rise early to spend time with God before your guests arrive. Pray for them by name.

- Think about your guests ahead of time: What are their interests? What foods do they like or dislike? If necessary, write down some questions that you will ask them during the mealtime.

A Restful Place

*You're always at home
in the Father's heart.*

Create a Place for Storage

"Where is your storage place?" Jesus asked, stepping into my front foyer.

Thinking He meant the place I kept all my junk, I pointed to the attic. We had been so eager to buy a house, that we failed to notice it had no hall closet or additional storage—only some shelves for linen down the hall. Limited space forced us to stuff thirty years of accumulations into a few small bedroom closets, kitchen cabinets, and a bulging attic. Boxes filled with childhood toys, nostalgic memorabilia, Christmas decorations, tax records, and junk—lots of junk—lined the walls of this collectaholic's attic.

Jesus shook His head, then looked at my empty hall tree standing in the front hallway. And then I knew what He meant. Years ago, my father had given that hall "holding" tree to me— one of the antique oak furnishings discarded from his office at work. On Daddy's own hall tree at home and on every doorknob, nail, or hook in his bedroom hung his weathered hats and wrinkled clothes. When my dad finished working in the yard or on an antique car, he would promptly deposit his stained pants and faded work shirts on the nearest "hang up" spot—for repeated wear the next day (or until Mom could sneak them out for laundering).

After my father's death a few years ago, Mom returned a few of Daddy's hats to me—some I had given him years before as gifts. Now my hall tree holds one of the hats he once hung in the foyer of his home.

In a sense, the branches of that "tree" symbolized a restful holding place where I could store my prayers, memories, and concerns. Whenever I passed by that oak structure, I remembered particularly the times we prayed for my father. For over twenty years, we deposited prayers for his health—from the first heart attack until his last heartbeat. The first time he literally passed from life to death to life again. It was only a minute—sixty seconds—but I'm sure it seemed like eons to my mom until the doctors shocked his heart back into an even rhythm. A few years later another attack followed, but again he survived.

Shortly after Dad's early retirement, the doctors discovered a blockage following a routine catheterization. My father needed open-heart surgery. I asked God, "Like the biblical King Hezekiah, please give Daddy at least fifteen more years."

My father's schedule slowed down somewhat, but God answered our prayers and gave him more time. He still managed to pastor and help smaller churches for several years. But eventually Daddy's heart began to weaken. Even a pacemaker couldn't help.

One sunny day on the front lawn, Daddy stooped down to inspect the front flowerbed. When Mom found him, his six-foot-four frame lay prone on their manicured lawn. Mother, holding him in her arms, tried to help him up, but his strength had vanished. A man who had always believed "I can" whispered to her, "I. . .just. . .can't. . .make. . .it." And then he was gone.

So live that your memories will be a part of your happiness.

ANONYMOUS

Like many who struggle with grief, my system shut down for a time in shock. Questions flooded like a river: "Why didn't I call sooner?" "Why did he have to leave this world so soon?" "Could I have done more to help?" And memories of the past rushed to my mind as I replayed the tapes of childhood, teenage, and adult years.

I had hung some of those memories on the hall tree. One was from a Christmas a few years before Daddy died. Not known for extravagant gifts (Daddy was quite frugal—we kidded him for being "tight"), his gift to us kids that Christmas caught us off guard. It wasn't the cost—in dollars—but the time spent in preparing that gift that meant so much. As the family gathered together for the grand opening, my father mysteriously disappeared and returned with a tape recorder. Then, with our mouths gaping open and tears trickling down our faces, we listened to our "gift."

When we were children, Daddy had a habit of sneaking in a tape recorder on special occasions. Often he would encourage us to ham it up, sing a favorite tune, or recite our Christmas wish list. Daddy had first recorded the tapes on a wire spool. He enlisted a professional to transfer one of those old tapes to a reel-to-reel recorder, then finally onto a cassette.

As I listened to my own preschool ramblings on that tape

> *You do not have to be rich to be generous. If he has the spirit of true generosity, a pauper can live like a prince.*
>
> CORINNE U. WELLS

at our family gathering, I realized how many years had passed since my childhood. I wondered then how many more times God would bless our holidays with a complete family circle. Unfortunately, not enough.

Only one more Christmas arrived where the entire family gathered with Daddy present. As each of us took turns that last year sharing what had been our favorite Christmas, I heard my father echo what had easily become mine—the Christmas when he had given each of us that childhood tape. As is so often true, the giver always gains a greater blessing than the receiver—but in this case, I think it was a tie.

When my father died, he didn't leave an abundance of personal belongings. Among my cherished treasures are one of his Bibles, a batch of his best sermons, his barely legible, handwritten letters to me, a hat or two, a flannel shirt I snuggle up in on cold days, a few other trinkets—and a tape that spelled love T-I-M-E.

Perhaps that gift was Daddy's way of making up for all the times when ministry pulled him away from family—when someone else's crisis needed his attention—or when yet another meeting demanded his leadership. At any rate, it was one of his best gifts.

Through the years our "holding tree" had become even more than a storage place for prayers and memories. That piece of furniture symbolized a place to hang my heart. It represented a place where, along with damp umbrellas and hats, I could hang up my worries to dry temporarily—a place where my Heavenly Father held out loving arms any day, anytime. There, like a giant oak tree, He gave me shade, comfort, and a peglike branch to "hang out" my cares and concerns for awhile.

_____

Surely Jesus knew I had used this storage place well. *Had.* But what about the worries and concerns of recent years? Perhaps I had stuffed too many things into the attic of my mind. Had I given fear an entrance and courted worry right into my home, bypassing the front hall tree? Like the biblical Sarah, who devised her own scheme to birth a son instead of waiting on the Lord, I, too, had exchanged God's plans for my own agenda in the last few years. As a result, confidence faltered, worries mounted, and my "attic" sagged with stacked-up burdens. And in stark contrast, the hall tree stood naked, stripped of its purpose for existence.

I looked into Jesus' eyes. He was waiting for my answer. Slowly, deliberately, like a child carefully decorating a Christmas tree with glass ornaments, I began to hang one burden at a time upon the old antique hall tree—until every peg was almost bending beneath the weight. Suddenly, I felt lighter. A load had lifted, and I was ready to continue our tour.

_____

When life needs a "holding place," where do you go? Do your arms tire of heavy loads? Have you hidden painful memories and misplaced happier ones?

As wives, moms, and friends, we also become caretakers of others' burdens. What woman hasn't on more than one occasion cried, "Enough!"? What better refuge than to run to our Father's arms? There we can rest without our burdens until we're strong enough to complete our journey. There, we're always at home.

> *"Come to me, all you who are weary and burdened, and I will give you rest."*
>
> MATTHEW 11:28 NIV

But the best thing about letting God be our holding tree is what we find later on our way out the front door—or what we *don't* find. Reaching over to pick up our wet tears and wrinkled worries again, we discover those items we hung up have been removed already by a caring Heavenly Father. Hanging there instead we see fresh promises for our journey. The old memories are there, but they have been washed and dried—sweetened with the softening hand of a gentle Savior.

We will be wise not to go digging in the closet for new burdens to carry.

Master Designer Secret

Cast all your anxiety on him because he cares for you.
1 PETER 5:7 NIV

Heart Check

*Where do you hang your memories
and worries to dry?*

A TRIBUTE TO DAD

*He's a giant of a man, with big, strong hands
    that hold your heart in his own.
The words he speaks are apples of gold—
    that can melt a heart of stone.
His laugh is contagious—His smile sincere;
His life is a book read far and near.
His love gives generous helpings to all;
For a father, you see, is always on call.
His thoughts are old-fashioned, and sometimes his clothes;
But godliness clothes him—from his head to his toes.
He has numerous flaws, which he often speaks of,
    but his family is blind and covers in love.
Long after he's gone, a sweet legacy stays
    filling the hearts of his family with praise.*

A Protected Place

*With the light of God's love
and protection from above,
home is a haven on earth.*

Add Proper Lighting

On a simple wood table in my front hall foyer sits a small group of angels and candles along with this quote by Henry Rische:

> *This home is a lighthouse which has the lamp of God on the table and the light of Christ in the window, to give guidance to those who wander in darkness.*[1]

That's one of my desires for our home: to radiate light, like a candle, into the lives of those who live here and those who visit.

I love candles. Throughout the year my favorite floral scents of rose, gardenia, vanilla, and mulberry fill the house. Scented candles grace every room of our home, not just on the hallway table. Each afternoon before Larry returns from work, when my grown children come home for a visit, or before expected guests arrive, I light a candle. There's something about the aroma that reminds me to take notice: A special moment is about to happen. To me, it's the fragrance of love—and a tradition I plan to keep.

And although I don't collect them, I love angels. Each time I look at one, God reminds me of all the times our family has felt the brush of angel wings—times of impending danger or, as Rische says, times of "wandering in darkness."

I remember one such moment as a sophomore in high school. My husband, Larry, and I were teenage sweethearts at the time, and we had been dating about a year. Our church association owned a special camp near a lake about ten miles outside of town. One night the youth department had planned a Hawaiian luau. I borrowed an authentic grass skirt (a souvenir from Larry's dad's war days in the Philippines) to wear over my own clothes with a colorful, flowered blouse. We ate shish kebabs with so much pineapple, we almost burned the taste buds off our tongues from the acid. But the night was a huge success.

A few months later, another couple, June and Weldon, double-dated with us to a valentine sweetheart banquet. After the banquet, we spontaneously decided to cruise out to the lakeside luau spot for a quick look. The encampment was closed, so we drove past. Larry was trying to tune in the radio to our favorite hit song, and he failed to see the approaching stop sign. That sign signaled the intersection of a major highway.

As we flew through the intersection without stopping, I remember looking up and seeing two bright mammoth eyes speeding toward us. In a split second, a pickup truck hit us broadside, just behind Larry on the driver's side. We spun around like kids on an amusement park ride and landed in a ditch on the side of the road. The impact left the door on Larry's shiny, black Plymouth Fury badly crushed and inoperable. As soon as we crawled out on the passenger side, Larry hugged me and checked the other couple with us. As the darkness engulfed us, we were still in shock.

Within a few minutes, an older woman emerged from a field of weeds like a mystical character from the movie *Field of Dreams* and escorted June and me to her house about a hundred yards away. Our dates waited to talk with the highway patrolman and the driver of the pickup truck who hit us.

In the light of the woman's modest home, I gasped as I looked at June. Small drops of blood were trickling down her face and hands from some minor cuts. But as she shook her turquoise taffeta dress, a hundred minuscule fragments of glass sprinkled to the floor. In the backseat, the window had shattered and sprayed glass in June's hair, her dress, and even her slip. A few spots of blood blended in with my red chiffon skirt, but for the most part I had only a bruised knee and a small cut on my finger.

"See, I am sending an angel ahead of you to guard you along the way and to bring you to the place I have prepared."

EXODUS 23:20 NIV

We found out later that except for a few punctures that needed stitches and some other light cuts and bruises, we all fared well. Some unseen angels must have been at work that night. The highway patrolman who investigated the accident just shook his head as he looked at the twisted wreckage. "Son, a few more inches. . .and. . .well, I hope you realize you all could have been killed."

Since that night, we've experienced many more "close calls," each time with an awareness that invisible eyes watched nearby. One particular time our family encountered what we considered to be our favorite kind of angel—the flesh and blood kind.

While on the way to Colorado one summer, we somehow took a wrong turn near Farmington, New Mexico. In the middle of nowhere, our faithful "Old Yeller" Chevrolet spewed out a series of *chugga-chuggas* as we eased over to the shoulder of the busy highway. We prayed and asked God to send someone to help us. Psalm 91 had been our vacation psalm for years, and we were counting on its promises once again. When we looked up, we noticed a small sign just down and across the road from us: "Midway Body Shop."

Larry opened the car door and walked up to a trailer on the small lot. After showing the middle-aged woman his business card and convincing her he was not a thief or mugger, she invited him in to use the phone. Ten or more calls later, still no help on the horizon. Suddenly the woman motioned for Larry to follow her. Stepping out back, she called her son-in-law, Juan, who worked as a mechanic in a body shop behind her home. Juan lifted the hood of our car and pronounced his conclusion: "Just a broken rocker arm." He found an engine in his shop just like "Old Yeller's" with a working rocker arm and an accompanying push rod. But he still needed another part: a valve cover.

For the next two hours until sundown, Larry and Juan

scoured the town, but no shops carried the part. During that time together, Larry discovered some missing parts of Juan's heart as well. Larry listened, gently encouraging Juan to release his bitterness.

While the two hunted in town, Juan's mother-in-law stuffed the girls and me full of tuna fish sandwiches, fresh fruit, and plentiful conversation. Time passed quickly, and soon the two men returned. Juan, relentless in his search, continued to poke around in his garage. When he returned, we couldn't believe what he had found in a hidden corner of his body shop: a set of valve covers that exactly fit our old 1978 Chevrolet.

Juan refused any money for his labor, insisting that *we* were the angels who had blessed *him*. That night after he repaired our car, we all held hands—his family and ours.

In the dim light of that tiny garage, I thought how much we could use the light of a candle—for light and for celebration. But then as I looked up, I fully expected Juan to sprout

It is impossible to give yourself away and not receive something back in the process.

wings before my eyes. For I could have sworn I saw a halo of light—faint but visible—circling Juan's head. And wafting through the smell of grease and oil was the distinct odor of heaven's sweet fragrance—the rose of Sharon.

⟨꙰⟩

"It's time," Jesus said.

"Time for what?" I was clueless. Here was a special place

I had already prepared soon after moving in. What change was needed here? Thinking Jesus meant it was time to light a candle to welcome my husband home, I ran to the kitchen for a match. But a glance at the clock revealed several hours still remained before Larry would return. I took the matches anyway and pulled one out to light a candle. But when I lowered the match to the candles, I couldn't light them. I had burned them down to the bare metal band. There was no wick—and no way—to light my candles.

Embarrassed, I stole a quick look at Jesus, who was smiling knowingly. And then He moved on.

"I am the light of the world."

JOHN 8:12 NIV

"Wait!" I cried. "I'm not ready for the rest of our walk-through yet. Let me get some new candles." I scurried to the pantry and looked for some new sources of fuel. But there were none. I would need a trip to Wal-Mart.

For a moment I felt like one of the high priest's sons in the Old Testament tabernacle who had shirked his duties. Aaron and his sons were to keep the lamps burning in the Holy Place all night long (Exodus 27:21). The light in that seven-candled lampstand was representative of the Lord's presence. The oil, a product of olives beaten and pressed like the Lord Jesus Himself, symbolized the Spirit of the Lord that would one day burn brightly in the hearts of all believers.

As keeper of the house—and Christ's tabernacle, my heart—how could I give light to those in darkness when there was no wick—no oil—in my lamp?

He had already provided His angels for my protection. But

what if He needed my "angel-with-skin-on" help as well, for those who were "wandering in darkness"? And hadn't I been given the privilege of sharing my light with others—not with my own puny wick of self-driven efforts, but through the power of God's Holy Spirit within me? It had been awhile since someone saw the light in my window and on my table.

I made a note to buy new candles as soon as our tour was finished. And then I hurried on to catch up with Jesus, eager to see what other renovations lay ahead.

Master Designer Secret

Blessed are those. . .
who walk in the light
of your presence,
O Lord.

PSALM 89:15 NIV

Heart Check

Is your candle:
(1) burning brightly?
(2) flickering
(3) out of "oil"?

Loving Touches

Many who have been stranded on
their journey in life
will testify to encounters with angels.
These silent friends may not bear wings,
but after they have passed,
the fluttering of our hearts bears witness
to another of heaven's miracles.

KEEP THE FIRE GLOWING

For special occasions when you want to add warmth to the living room (but not excessive heat), place an arrangement of candles, all shapes and sizes, inside your fireplace. Close the screen, and keep the fire glowing, even in springtime!

A Contented Place

Home may be a cottage
or a castle on a hill;
it's love that makes a house a home,
and Christ who makes it real.

Use Natural Colors

As I look back, I realize my heart has always yearned for a simple style that whispered, "Rebecca." For the first few years of our marriage, we furnished our homes with "Shabbier Chic." I worked outside my home for almost four years until our first baby was born. Subsequently, choosing the life of a stay-at-home mom after that meant eliminating luxuries and concentrating on the basic necessities.

Our first big purchases were a $39.95 kitchen table and an $11.00 television set, a great buy from a nearby auction. I also inherited my grandmother's bed and hope chest.

All of these fit perfectly into our otherwise furnished sixteen-by-sixteen-foot box cottage. When the West Texas winds blew in Abilene, where we attended college, the wallpaper flapped in perfect rhythm with the sounds of the creaking hardwood floors. Our first rented place was simple—but it felt like home.

Ten years later, we finally purchased a modest new house. My decor mirrored a mixture of my friends' tastes: a blend of cutesy country, Southwestern basketry, and art wacko. After all, variety is the spice of life. Other fashionable friends covered my ignorance by calling my style "eclectic." Actually, it looked more like hectic. Still, it was home. And this time, all the furnishings belonged to us.

Another decade passed, and we moved to the Dallas area, where home furnishings looked more like Ethan Allen than Fred Sanford. Somehow we landed a beautiful four-bedroom, two-story home. With a small sum from the sale of our previous house, I bought a few things in my favorite color: blue. But I had no clue how to decorate this too-big, half-empty house.

I had netted a few good antique purchases at a couple of garage sales years ago: a six-foot pine armoire and an oak icebox. I fashioned drapes for the huge living room windows out of mauve and blue sheets and watched for craft and garage sales to dress the empty walls.

I had never taken an interior decorating class. My girls had even accused me of being color-blind. But each time people walked through the door of our home, they remarked how *homey* and *warm* our house felt. I wasn't sure if that was a put-down or a compliment. But I loved that house.

Then we moved about three years ago to a smaller town about forty-five minutes from the Dallas metroplex. We chose to downsize, but practicality ruled out the Victorian, wrap-around porch-style home of my

I saw that wisdom is better than folly, just as light is better than darkness.

ECCLESIASTES
2:13 NIV

dreams. No one built log cabins in the city limits, so we opted for a medium-size house much smaller than our previous one. I had looked forward to discovering—and decorating—with my own style and personality, perhaps for the first time ever.

Through the years, we had accepted invitations to use special friends' lakeside cottages and retreats for vacations and had even contributed our meager skills to help build a Colorado mountain hideaway for our dear friends Chet and Millie Daniel. Millie had given me some copies of *Victoria* magazine a few years earlier. I had been forming the perfect atmosphere for my home. Mentally, I poured over those peaceful hideaways and from all those pictures pieced together the scraps of ideas for decorating my Victorian city cottage.

That was before Jesus challenged my ideas. Now I had just exchanged my own designer blueprints for Christ's renovations. Where was He leading me now?

───♏

When I caught up with Jesus, He was staring at the walls. "Natural colors work best," He offered mysteriously.

I scratched my head in confusion. "But the walls *are* painted in neutral colors—except those with wallpaper. See?" I said smugly, pointing to each wall. "Light—and bright!"

Wait a minute. Did He say neutral or natural? One look at Jesus and I had my answer.

Once again those piercing eyes saw clear through my soul. It reminded me of another time years ago when others' eyes penetrated my disguises, revealing my natural colors.

It was a harmless charade. All of the youth workers donned their favorite disguises and hid in the local mall, while the youth in our church tried to find us. The winner? The one who uncovered the most disguises.

I chose the guise of a pregnant mom, stuffing a pillow inside my skirt and blouse for proper effect. Then I waddled my way down the aisle of a department store, hoping to blend in with the other shoppers.

Not long after, the kids began racing through the mall, sniffing out their targets like junior bloodhounds. Once a man happened to be standing near me. One of the youth tapped him on the shoulder apologetically. "Excuse me, uh, excuse me, Sir!" Then pointing to me, the teen asked, "Is that your wife?"

The man took one look at my condition, threw up his arms, and shouted in alarm, "No! That's not *my* wife!"

Other young teens approached me timidly and asked, "Excuse me. Don't you go to my church?"

The youth of our church eventually saw through all our disguises. Maybe they figured out *my* natural colors because of my tilted blond wig, the "shifting" baby, or the dark sunglasses I wore at 8:00 P.M.

A few years later, I tried another ruse, this time of my own doing. I approached the cosmetics counter of a well-known department store and I let my fingers do the talking. I was a beginning church deaf interpreter and had been taking classes to improve my skills. I had hoped to increase my sensitivity to the deaf culture as well, so I pretended to be deaf. Perhaps in this way I could see the difficulty of communicating without words.

The saleswoman understood my request, and I bagged my cosmetics. I felt smug that I had pulled it off like some robbery heist—until the next week when I returned to purchase a new "milk masque." To my total embarrassment, the same clerk appeared and remembered my "deafness." My first lie had led me to yet another cowardly deception. At one point I forgot and opened my mouth to answer the woman's question, then quickly coughed to cover my error, hoping she hadn't noticed.

Those harmless charades led me not to a greater understanding of others and myself but to a deeper discontentment of who I was. Growing up a minister's daughter in a fishbowl life had not affected me too adversely, or so I thought. As a ninety-nine-pound, five foot-nine twelve-year-old, I disliked my inherited, physical genes. Each time I'd look in the mirror, I would pretend I saw a shapely model—*not* the "string bean" I was labeled by my classmates. When people would walk by and ask, "How tall *are* you?" I politely resisted the urge to respond, "How *short* are you?"

> *What makes us special is not our body but the signature of God on our lives.*
>
> MAX LUCADO,
> *In the Grip of Grace*

Early in our ministry, one woman approached me and commented, "You don't *look or act* like a typical minister's wife." I didn't know what a typical minister's wife was supposed to look—or act—like, but I determined to find out. So, for the next few years, I began to try on the "hats" of other women, just to see if they fit. Perhaps God wanted me to wear a "happy," youthful, denim hat and be the smiling minister's wife who never threw fits in front of the deacons, spoke a cross word to her husband, or voted for blue carpet in business meetings when everyone else wanted green. So I tried that. And it worked for awhile—until I also decided it was my duty to play "Patch Adams" and be responsible for everyone else's happiness. When that backfired, I stuffed the happy hat back in the closet!

Then I looked around at other bold ministers' wives and thought, *Maybe God wants me to take a stronger leadership role.* So I grabbed a take-charge hat and stood behind the podium with a microphone in my hand—and a quiver in my liver. In time, I learned I could actually lead fairly well. But was this what God wanted?

Later, I thought, *I know! I envy those women whose personalities never change, the ones who are always in the "Word." The ones who constantly wave some dazzling new truth from Scripture in front of you.* So I dug out a floppy garden hat to remind me to stay green and growing spiritually. There was one small problem. I had PMS. Not your type "A" general malaise PMS. I often called mine "pre-monster syndrome." My family readily agreed. How can one remain unruffled and consistent with hormones raging out of control like a runaway roller coaster?

Alas! Wouldn't I love to be like that woman who holes herself up in some romantic cottage creating works of art and letting her pen be the microphone of her soul? So I donned my wide-brimmed, floral Southern hat and tried to squeeze creative

54

moments in between mounds of fluffy, mashed potatoes and Downy-soft laundry. Guilty thoughts of *Am I doing enough in the church?* often interrupted the flow of creativity, however. *Would I ever discover what a minister's wife should do or be?*

Not only had I often tried on others' hats to find my place in life, but I had also fallen into the deadly habit of comparison. I know I'm not alone. How many of us have played that game at one time or another? "Just look at her body. She's a perfect 10! I'm a perfect—16!" "Her children never throw things in public." "Her house could be featured in *Country Living* magazine." "Her lasagna never burns."

> *My business is not to remake myself, but make the absolute best of what God made.*
>
> ROBERT BROWNING

Through the years I had learned to be more content with my physical appearance, but I still struggled at times with my God-given abilities (or lack of them). My friend Beverly played the piano like a virtuoso. I played, too, but the music minister only called me in emergencies. Beverly was a vivacious blond. I was a warm brunette. She was good with people. I was good with words. When someone more skilled than I would appear on the scene, I retreated in self-consciousness.

Occasionally, the comparisons still sneak in and catch me off guard. A few years ago I was asked to speak at a large women's retreat in another state and was excited about the approaching date—until I realized one of my friends and fellow coauthors, Becky Freeman, had spoken there the year before. Immediately, I saw caution lights and roadblocks.

"God!" I pleaded. "Why did You ask me to go speak there? Becky is an accomplished humorist. When she walks up to the podium, people start laughing. But when I take the microphone, people start passing the Kleenex!"

Silence. Then, God spoke inaudibly. "Your point is?"

"Well, Lord, my point is, she's funny!" I continued. When I insisted to my husband a few years ago that I could be funny, too, he told me, "Rebecca, you're either funny or you're not funny. And, Honey," he said, "you're *not* funny!" He was referring to the way I told jokes—another of those gifts from my dad. My jokes were like a train without a caboose. Like my father, I would consistently forget the punch line.

Larry and I made a bet. "I'll show you I can be funny," I said. When five of us women agreed to write two humor books, I won. Becky, Gracie, Fran, Suzie, and I had actually managed to laugh our way through both books writing light-hearted stories of our own. At the end of those sessions, when the final products were released, I held up the proof. "See? Humor!" to which he readily conceded. But most of my writing and speaking felt more like the passion of Elizabeth Barrett Browning.

Again I asked God why He chose me for the retreat. Again, silence. Then I heard the Lord speak to my heart. "Rebecca, this weekend retreat is not about you. It's about Me. And it's about those women. I chose you because I like using weak and broken vessels."

"Thanks a lot," I interrupted.

"And because there is something I want those women to

hear—from you. Now will you just go and be yourself?"

So I did. And as always, God was faithful to show up.

⟶

My Master Designer seemed to be reading my thoughts. "Only one thing is needful," He reminded me gently, as He would do repeatedly throughout our tour.

"My grace is sufficient for you, for my power is made perfect in weakness."

2 CORINTHIANS 12:9 NIV

I thought again of Mary and Martha and of my first conversation with Jesus at the front door of my home. These two women were different. But both had valid gifts and unique personalities. Jesus hadn't said to Martha, "I wish you were more like Mary. She's the kind of woman you need to mirror. Your hospitality gifts serve no purpose to Me." Nor did He rebuke Mary by saying, "Mary, why can't you set a table and cook like Martha?"

I believe what Jesus did say between the lines was, "Martha, no one sets a more beautiful table than you. But if you're going to wear yourself out preparing, if it means we must use Lenox china and Oneida silverware, that you stay up half the night just to serve Me dinner, and you're so irritable that you can't even enjoy your company, then Martha, something is wrong. I would rather eat cheese and crackers, Martha, and dine on the simple joy of your presence. Mary could serve, too, but let Mary be Mary. You be Martha, but choose a different attitude—a heart that makes time for her

Lord and her guests, that cares more for the people than the preparations. Be yourself, Martha, but remember the relationship."

Throughout the Bible, Jesus treated people as individuals with their own gifts and abilities. By the very uniqueness of His methods and approach to others, He said to them, "There is no one else like you."

Isaiah 45:9 reminds us, "Does the clay say to the potter, why did you make me this way?" (NIV with author's paraphrase). No, "Lord. . .We are the clay, you are the potter. . ." (Isaiah 64:8 NIV).

You may be arguing, "I'm a chipped vessel, and I'm holding the pieces of my broken heart to prove it. I'm no longer useful to God."

But if you're content to simply be yourself, your life will count for plenty.

MATTHEW 23:12
THE MESSAGE

The prophet Jeremiah added his thoughts to the subject: "But the pot he was shaping from the clay was marred in his hands"; *so the potter threw it away. No. So the potter decided to use another pot. No.* "So the potter formed it into another pot, shaping it as seemed best to him" (Jeremiah 18:4 NIV).

What will it take for you to be content with your worth as a woman? A better paying job? Smarter children or grandchildren? A better home? More friends? More applause? Visible results of your ministry? Better health?

Listen to Jesus as He gently whispers, "Do you not know you are that piece on the potter's wheel, and I am not finished with you yet? Be still and let me make you into who you were created to be. And be content with who you are."

As a minister's wife, I spent half my life trying to live up to what I thought other people wanted me to be—and to my own expectations. I sighed, grateful for the reminder to be content.

⁀

Since that time, I have felt a newfound freedom—with my Designer's blessing—to move ahead and discover some of my "natural colors." I disliked the formal look of gold and velvets, but lace, rich greens, and burgundies shouted, "Yes!" Still reserving one room for blue and white, I again made my furniture purchases from some of the house proceeds.

I selected carefully, taking my time to complete each room. I knew this would probably be my only major buying spree—and for the first time in my life, I understood my heart's longings.

My children were grown, so I worked from room to room like an artist with a palette, painting the mental images I had collected. This time, we chose a few sturdier pieces—ones that were symbols of my taste—inexpensive, but elegant. When one friend visited and said, "I've been in many homes —but when I walk in yours, it's so. . .peaceful," I knew I had found my simple retreat. I had a new desire to make my home a natural refuge, a restful place that had the peace of God on its walls and the love of God in our hearts. And I knew this was just a starting place with my Master Designer.

We've come a long way since those early days of college

and seminary when dinner consisted of Tuna Helper or fifteen-cent hamburgers. The children are gone, but the house is a refuge—fully furnished with precious memories from the past, promises for the future, and symbols of our simple desires. I can only hope that should God desire to remove our possessions, like Job, we would still feel blessed. We are just as happy as we were in the early days of our marriage—with or without things. But now, after designing my own simple furnishings, home means even more—and "happy" has changed to "contented."

No matter what furnishings you choose for your home, let them mirror your natural colors and radiate the simplicity and fragrance of Christ. You may not be able to afford expensive pieces, but you can create a loving atmosphere anywhere. Contentment knows it's the furnishings of the heart that make home "simply home."

—♋

"Rebecca." I heard a faint whisper. "It's time to move on." I was beginning to feel at home with Jesus. I only hoped my Master Designer felt the same way.

Master Designer Secret

*I've learned by now
to be quite content
whatever my circumstances.*

PHILIPPIANS 4:11 THE MESSAGE

Heart Check

Are you satisfied with your natural colors?

Loving Touches

SIMPLE PLAN

- Pray for God's help in designing your home and heart with natural colors—to make it a place of refuge—and a place where His heart—and yours—will feel at home.
- Start a "Dream" book. In a simple notebook binder, collect pictures from your favorite magazines, choosing house plan styles, color schemes, and furnishings you like.
- Begin a special savings account for both small and large purchases. Keep a record of your designated savings funds for home and furnishings purchases. Save for those sturdy

pieces of furniture that will eventually become your children and grandchildren's prized family treasures.

- Watch for special pieces at garage or estate sales or secondhand stores—even model home closeouts. With a little elbow grease and paint, you can create a beautiful treasure out of someone else's junk.

- Begin a journal of memories. Take a mental walk through the home(s) in which you grew up. What positive memories do you associate with each place? Then do the same with each room of your current house. Write down your remembrances.

A Warm, Loving Place

Nothing warms the heart more
than the flames of human kindness;
and nothing is as bright
as the light of God's love.

Keep the Fire Burning

We had listed our priorities ahead of time. Fireside chatter definitely ranked high on the list. When we first started looking for a house in our East Texas town, we had difficulty finding homes with fireplaces. For fifteen years we had sweltered under the sun's rays in Arizona. Before we moved back to Texas, we added a fireplace to our modest Arizona home. Some nights we literally had to crank up the air conditioner just to enjoy the flames. In our next home in the Dallas area, we enjoyed the coziness of another fireplace for about ten years.

How can I forget those cold Texas winters with my own husband and children—warming up to a crackling, blazing fire, a mug of hot apple cider in one hand, and a snack of popcorn or fudge brownies in the other? On holidays, especially at Christmas time in recent years, our family has gathered near the fire for our Christmas Eve fondue dinner. Laughter rang, and wood crackled while we speared yet another juicy morsel and popped it into our mouths. Later as we read again the familiar Christmas story of Christ's birth, our hearts

You are a king by your own fireside, as much as any monarch in his throne.

THEADORA VAN RUNKLE

warmed clear down to our toes.

When our children grew up and left home, our fireside chatter often turned to softer conversation. Like two pieces of finely aged wood, a middle-aged husband and wife rediscovered the sparks of new romance, and the warming of body and spirit beside the fireplace. Clearly, it is a place where we love to make—and celebrate—memories.

But if I look closely into the embers of that blazing fire of the past, I also see something else—a picture that takes me back to my childhood. My first recollections of a real fireplace were in Ridgecrest, North Carolina. I was about ten or eleven at the time, and our family had traveled there for a special conference and vacation. I had looked forward to the fertile, green mountain countryside—a stark contrast to our north Texas town at the time. But halfway to the conference center in Atlanta, Georgia, my face was flushed, my body feverish, and my neck swollen with a relapse of mumps.

After an emergency stop for medicine and a shot, we traveled on to our destination. And while everyone else attended the meetings, I lay cabin bound on the couch by the fireplace. My father wagged my autograph hound "Mustard" around the hillside, getting special speakers' autographs for me, while Mother read Tom Swift stories to me in front of a warm, toasty fireplace. She, too, missed out on the conferences. Not much fun for her, I'm sure, but I loved that fireplace chatter. And my love of books grew stronger.

Now as I gaze into the flames again, I see yet another fireside memory—this time several years later as a young mother. It was a simple celebration. Thanksgiving in Mexico brought no golden Butterball turkeys out of the oven, no creamy mashed potatoes, or savory herb dressing. But lots of beans, tortillas—and plenty of fireside chatter. Our family had traveled there as part of a larger church team to show Christian evangelistic movies in some of the villages and nearby churches.

One picture will haunt my memory forever. As we walked out of the humble church that cold evening, I looked next door at the flicker of a fire inside a tentlike structure—nothing more than a tiny hovel—six feet by six at the most. There, through the open door, I saw a bent figure—and two bony, wrinkled hands outstretched to catch the warmth of the smoldering fire. The firelight illuminated the old man's face, and I estimated him to be around eighty or eighty-five years old. A long scraggly beard hung down to his elbows. And the only fireside noise we heard was the chattering of crooked teeth—and the crackling of his small fire.

Later that week we projected our movies on a huge sheet on the basketball court—the only place large enough for crowds to see. There, I met Pedro, a seven-year-old Hispanic lad. It was forty degrees outside, and Pedro arrived barefoot in short sleeves and shorts. He huddled in my lap, jabbering away, and I loosened my warm wool coat to wrap around his body. Pedro hushed when the movie began and his shivering stopped. The only fireside chatter I heard that night was the Lord whispering to me, "If you do it for the least of these my brethren, you have done it unto me."

And so we returned to Mexico on several Thanksgiving

Whatever we hold to ourselves is loss. Whatever we give to God is gain.

GILBERT SHAW,
The Service of Love

holidays—each time receiving a greater blessing than the year before.

⁓

"To keep the fire burning, you'll need more wood," Jesus spoke softly, as He gazed at my empty fireplace.

Perhaps He was right. And I was catching on more quickly now to His method of renovations. His words made me wonder. Had the fire cooled in the recent winters of my heart? How long had it been since I had shared that fire with those whose hearts had grown cold and lifeless? How long since I walked with others through the heat of their own discontent and fanned the flames of hope in their hearts? Hadn't God done that for me?

There is a purifying that takes place in the flames of spiritual fire. Hearts, once hardened, melt from a stony mass to a liquid gold, eager to serve and love the very One who initiated the fire. And somehow there comes a quiet knowledge that recognizes, like Daniel and his friends in the fiery furnace, that God is always present—and at work—even in the fire.

My mind began to rehearse all the times our family walked through the fire, but emerged without so much as a singed hair or faint smell of smoke, for which I am most grateful. Even the times when we felt the heat turned up so high that our emotions and spirits sustained third-degree burns, the Master Controller allowed only what would melt away the superficial, the unnecessary, the useless. Through it all, He never left us.

⸺◌

As I place more wood in the fireplace, I do not see the face of Jesus like a shrine in the flames of my fire, but I feel the warmth and security of His love. And I know He will always be here to share this place with me.

We pause in our tour, pull up two chairs, and the fireside chatter we share is sweet and simple. For a moment, I take a deep breath, relax, and remember. . .and celebrate the awesome goodness of a great God.

⸺◌

Master Designer Secret

*He spread out. . .
a fire to give light at night.*

PSALM 105:39 NIV

Heart Check

*In the winter of your heart,
is there enough wood in the fireplace?*

Loving Touches

FIRESIDE MEMORIES

We left the comforts of home behind,
*   and eagerly set on our way;*
What we would do wasn't clear just yet,
*   or even the words we would say.*
The language and color were different from us,
*   yet something remained the same;*
The message of love and bond from above
*   ignited our hearts to a flame.*
We carried the name of Jesus to them—
*   some had never heard before;*
And the prayers of our people followed us there—
*   bold keys that opened the door.*
We painted, we swept, we walked, and we talked,
*   and the people responded so well;*
But the things that impressed us down deep in our hearts
*   are the hardest of all to tell.*
For the cardboard villages and barefoot children
*   left images hard to erase.*
And I still see them there, many standing threadbare,
*   with their hands reaching up to my face.*
And I knew the same Jesus I worshipped and loved
*   was here in this place as well.*
But the things that I saw and felt and heard
*   will always be hard to tell.*
I walked back into my luxurious home,
*   and thought, "Oh, it's good to be here."*
But the picture engraved on my heart was still clear
*   of the love-hungry people back there.*

A Transparent Place

*The pain of isolation
is far greater
than the pain of disclosure.*

Open the Curtains

It's too dark in here," said Jesus, as He looked around the room.

One of the things I did not like about our current house was the dark living room. Heavy foliage from the backyard trees filtered in little light. And the windows looked out directly through the covered patio—which darkened the room even more. Because of the numerous trees, which I loved, we could not see the sun rising each morning, and the brightness of the sun's rays stayed hidden throughout the day. I loved the rich oak color of the paneled walls and ceiling beams even though it was a style from the previous decade. I had seen others paint their wood panels a white or beige color to lighten it, but surely I could do something less drastic.

"Just open the curtains," Jesus spoke again.

I looked at the heavy thermal drapes. "But there is no window shade," I protested. "If I open the drapes all the way, others can see inside."

Silence. Then I saw it again. That knowing smile. *What did I say this time?*

*Who is
more foolish—
the child who
is afraid of
the dark,
or a man
who is afraid
of the light?*

ANONYMOUS

And then as if Jesus had opened the curtains of my own soul, He walked me back to a time when, not only had I closed the curtains of my life, but I had left others standing on the front porch of my heart. It wasn't that I had preferred the dark. It just didn't feel. . .safe. . .to open the door. And if I did invite someone in, I refused to throw back the curtains. Fear had closed the drapes; and fear had locked a corner of my heart.

⟶ ൦

Early in our ministry I learned a painful lesson. Thinking it was my spiritual assignment to make others happy, I put on my "fix-it" hat and went to work. But in the process I was hurt deeply—so deeply I decided to wipe *transparency* from my vocabulary for many years. I closed the curtains of my heart.

Those who knew me well actually only thought they did. I disguised the pain well, allowing a Pollyanna smile to cover a multitude of hurt. If anyone caught me in a panic attack or noted misty eyes, I had a ready excuse. PMS. Worked every time. Of course I held my breath, hoping no family member or friend ever noticed that my monthly malaise often lasted four weeks out of the month.

Perfection had been welded into my glass house mentality. Several well-meaning Christians had even confessed innocently to me over the years, "Christians aren't supposed to have problems, are they?"

Fear is a strange thing. Ryllis Lynip says, "Our greatest enemies are not wild beasts or deadly germs but fears that paralyze thought, poison the mind, and destroy character."[1] Like a venomous snake, fear fastens on to its victim with uncanny strength and refuses to let go. Women have told me, "I cannot release my unforgiveness. It is too hard." One woman said, "The shame of my affair is too great. I can never tell anyone." Another who was sexually abused as a child has lived with her secret for sixty years. Fear has stolen her desire to live, and she remains an emotional cripple. Still another one stores food treats in the corners of her refrigerator to indulge her secret addiction.

Because I refused to release the pain of my own hurt, depression overwhelmed me. One day it was so bad, I ran to the kitchen cabinet, grabbed a bottle of pills, and downed the entire bottle. The Lord has such a sense of humor. There were only two sinus tablets in that bottle! That same day, as I tried to sleep off my foolishness, the phone kept ringing. No one knew or even suspected my pain. Yet, people kept calling just to tell me they were praying for me or were thinking about me. Someone even placed a plant on my doorstep anonymously. Apparently God was sending out His angels on mission: "Go touch Rebecca. Go touch Rebecca."

During those months, I remember praying, "Lord, please send a mature woman my way. I need someone who understands!" *I* was supposed to be the mature woman. After all, I *was* the *minister's* wife. But I felt anything but mature. I thought my life was too broken for God to ever use again. But a Heavenly Father, in His gentle love and compassion, had a greater plan. Slowly, patiently, He drew me close again.

"Absolutely everything… as you make it a part of your believing prayer, gets included as you lay hold of God."

MATTHEW 21:22
THE MESSAGE

Sound familiar? Perhaps you're well acquainted with such traumas. Maybe you've been through a divorce, a best friend's betrayal, sexual abuse, an affair, drug or alcohol addiction. Maybe your children's lives are in shambles and you are feeling shame for them. And you've closed the curtains of your life, desperately trying to find protection again.

Perhaps you have been trying to touch the hem of Jesus' garment but find healing illusive and distant. You desperately want to be made whole—to open the curtains, to be real—but you're afraid. The words in Isaiah 42:3 NIV may offer encouragement to you: "A bruised reed he will not break, and a smoldering wick he will not snuff out." We are not beyond His reach. And just like the woman with a hemorrhage for twelve years, we can find hope in Jesus' words to her: "Daughter, your faith has healed you. Go in peace. . ." (Mark 5:34 NIV).

We need the touch of the Master, and we need the friendships, understanding, and safety of other women. We were not created to live in isolation. Jesus offers us a safe place, a calm retreat, a healing balm for broken hearts and lives.

After several years had passed, I finally shared my pain and received the help I needed to heal. Ultimately, my faithful heavenly Father's love restored beauty from the ashes of my life. In time, I began to understand a truth that I had often heard but had not really embraced.

Listen to the psalmist's words in Psalm 139:13–17 NIV:

For you created my inmost being;
you knit me together in my mother's womb.
I praise you because I am fearfully and wonderfully made;
your works are wonderful, I know that full well.
My frame was not hidden from you when I was made
in the secret place.
When I was woven together in the depths of the earth,
your eyes saw my unformed body.
All the days ordained for me were written in your book
before one of them came to be.
How precious to me are your thoughts, O God! How vast
is the sum of them!

When I began to understand God's unconditional love for me, I gained the courage to become transparent again to others—and they, too, reached out in love. Let me add that being real and transparent does not always mean sharing your pain with everyone. I have found there are at least two appropriate reasons God may impress you to do so: (1) for your own healing and (2) for someone else's healing.

Beth Moore reminds us of a beautiful principle in her Bible study, *Breaking Free.* When tragedy struck the Israelites and they slaved in captivity for so many years, they thought it was the end. Life was finished, and they could never wear their happy hats again. But on the night God helped them escape, the Egyptians literally gave the Israelites tons of loot, simply because they were so glad to see them go.

Ever wonder where the Hebrews got the gold, the

beautiful fabrics, all the material to build such an expensive tabernacle years later? From the spoils of their captivity—the Egyptians' gifts to them. They reinvested those treasures that came from such a dark period in their lives to build a beautiful, useful vessel of honor for the Lord.

Out of the trauma of some difficult years in our past, God has allowed my husband and me to reinvest our treasures of darkness—the lessons we learned. (And that's another chapter in itself.) We invested them into a passion for marriage, seeking to help strengthen and encourage other couples in their relationships. God gave me a personal desire to help others experience the Father's faithful and unconditional love for them. From those "spoils" of my own captivity, I made a lifelong commitment to know the Father's heart—and to help others do the same.

Beth Moore says, "Few people have grateful hearts like captives who have been freed and those afflicted who have been healed." Like many of you, I've been there and done that. And I just can't thank Jesus enough these days.

⌒

"Are you ready now?" Jesus asked softly. I loved His patience. Throughout our tour He waited on me while my thoughts wandered. But then, He who knows our thoughts also controls and directs our thoughts. As we walked through the house, I wondered, *Is it He who is stirring my memory?* Was He the one seeding my thoughts with reminders of His faithfulness?

"Ready for what?" I quizzed Him. I glanced over at the

closed drapes, where His eyes were still focused.

Guarded transparency had not troubled me once my emotional healing began years ago. But I was much older now and in yet another house, another place, and another season of my life. Occasionally, old fears submerged. It was easier to bury pain and never speak of it again. But as I looked at Jesus, He reached out a compassionate and tender hand and led me over to the living room drapes. Together, we slowly opened the curtains again. In fact, months later, I even purchased new drapes —thin, transparent ones that remain open twenty-four hours a day. Of course, I also bought a shade for nighttime. Even Jesus needed privacy.

In doing that, God showed me a third reason for being wisely transparent: (3) to show God's awesome power of restoration, beauty, and healing—and to prove His love and faithfulness to a doubting world. And how faithful He has been to me!

When God gave His Son to die for us, He proved once and for all just how much He loved us. And as an eight-year-old child, I embraced that love for the first time. But through the years I often forgot the magnitude and security of that love. One day Jesus gave me a beautiful object lesson, as if to say once more, "I did it for you!"

"Keep open house; . . . By opening up to others, you'll prompt people to open up with God."

MATTHEW 5:16
THE MESSAGE

I'll tell you about it in the next chapter.

Master Designer Secret

*What you're after is
truth from the inside out.*

PSALM 51:6 THE MESSAGE

Heart Check

*Have you allowed God to reinvest
the spoils of your captivity?*

Loving Touches

LET THE SUN SHINE IN

White curtains are brighter and will reflect more light, giving
you a sharper contrast to the other colors in the room.

- Choose the fabric according to the amount of light you
  want in your room.
- Sheer or lace curtains will give you a full window view
  and filtered light. Heavier, insulated curtains will block
  the light.
- Tieback curtains will also allow more light and actually
  give a visual widening effect. Tie them back wherever

you wish to bring in various amounts of light.

OTHER DECORATING TIPS

- To darn small holes or tears in lace curtains, place a piece of netting dampened with starch over the holes on the wrong side and then press it down firmly with a hot iron.
- Roll a marble through the casing of a freshly ironed curtain, and the rod will slip through easily.
- If you have a collection of old keys, use them to weight down hems of your drapes. [III]

A Secure Place

*The treasures of the heart
cannot be measured monetarily.
Who can say what love is worth?*

Display Valuables Prominently

Each time I walked into my mother's living room, one corner lured me repeatedly. Like many women, Mother kept her delicate breakables and beautiful china in a glass hutch. I had admired her collection for years and loved running my fingers over the smooth, satiny curves and lines of each piece. Each one represented a colorful glass garden to me: ruby roses, purple heathers, turquoise irises, and sunny yellow daffodils. I owe much of my appreciation of beautiful things to my mother's tastes and love of fine dishes.

But one day after I was grown, I was home visiting Mother. As I walked to the corner of her living room, I noticed on the top shelf of my mom's hutch, nestled in the middle of some exquisite glass, a strange-looking art piece. Fashioned by eleven-year-old fingers years before, it was a crude clay elephant holding its trunk, with tears trickling down a wrinkled face. I had shaped that small figure in Mrs. Ehlert's sixth-grade art class and presented it to Mom on Mother's Day. Little did I know then what significance that tearful mammal would hold for me years later.

With one small act, Mother had said volumes to me. It was as if this little "elephant in a china shop" had found a home in her heart. Mother had no idea, but at that time in my life the words "I can't" paralyzed my own spiritual journey. My insecurity as a young minister's wife dominated my thinking. I had gradually allowed others' expectations—and my own —to replace the truth of God's Word about my self-worth.

But Mom's prominent placement of that homely elephant spelled love and value to this struggling woman in search of her identity. Just like Jesus returning to His heavenly home to prepare a place for His children, my mother had "prepared the place" for me by including a piece of my heart in her beautiful collections.

> *The greatest happiness of life is the conviction that we are loved—loved for ourselves, or rather, loved in spite of ourselves.*
>
> VICTOR HUGO

Years later, my mom began the steady process of disbursing some of those glass treasures back to me. Along with other childhood goodies, I buried that piece of clay in my "treasure" chest of drawers—often forgetting the lesson it taught me.

⁓

"Remember the elephant?" I heard Jesus say. "Where is it?"

His reminder to me sent me digging. Perhaps that little elephant's tears were symbolic of the gratitude its designer would feel years later. Because now in my kitchen, on the top shelf of my wooden hutch, cradled by a small collection of antique glass and dishes, sits that crude clay elephant. That small animal is a symbol that I am loved and cherished for who I am not only by my mom, but also by my Creator and Master Designer, who helped fashion me into the woman I am today. It was God who ultimately determined my worth and value long before my birth. It was He who stamped "Original" on my blueprints and ordained my days to include purposeful living and joyful giving.

And that little painted elephant reminds me that the simple treasures in life are not expensive accumulations. More valuable than the most exquisite art glass is the priceless inheritance of being His heavenly child, the simple privilege of being valued by a Father who accepts me and loves me unconditionally, who has elevated me to His top shelf—all because of genuine love.

"Why would He do that?" you ask. Why would God station us in a place of prominence? Because God "raised us up together, and made us sit together in the heavenly places in Christ Jesus" (Ephesians 2:6 NKJV). Why? So that in the future "He might show the exceeding riches of His grace in His kindness toward us in Christ Jesus" (v. 7). Christ, too, is raised up in heavenly places—and God has placed us there beside Him—in a prominent place where we can be seen by all. Why? Because He wants to display His grace and love through us!

You may say, "I'm not in a prominent place. I think God forgot about this homely piece of clay. I've been in the background for years. No one knows—or even cares—what I do."

God does. It's not where we serve that qualifies us for

that prominent place. It's where He has elevated us in His heart. And that is what makes us valuable—not what we do, but who we are in Christ. There is nothing more life changing than to know that we are totally, unconditionally loved and accepted by God.

And we are.

Master Designer Secret

The Lord has chosen you to be his treasured possession.

DEUTERONOMY 14:2 NIV

Heart Check

In God's eyes, how much are you worth?
Have you received His total, unconditional love?

Loving Touches

THE POTTER'S TREASURE

You are His special treasure,
once a broken piece of clay—
now shaped with care and fashioned

to His utmost perfection.
You are His pride and joy,
not a discarded toy from play—
but destined for His pleasure,
the prize of the Potter's collection.

A Joyful Place

Blessed is the home adorned with love, joy, and peace.

Add Generous Splashes of Color

After Jesus' reminder to be myself and that He loves me just as I am, I was feeling very secure. But His next words opened up another question mark in my mind.

Looking around at the walls, floors, and furnishings, He said, "Don't forget to add generous splashes of color."

Another decorator principle I already knew. When you use neutral—and natural—colors throughout your home, you can easily bring out colorful touches with pillows, pictures, rugs, flower arrangements, and various accessories placed here and there. But I had done that. In fact, I had immersed my home with color. In the living room, I had chosen colorful burgundy couches with natural accents. On the walls and scattered throughout the house were beautiful splashes of colorful prints and accessories designed by my favorite artist, Glynda Turley.

"But there *is* color here," I protested.

Then Jesus did something totally foreign to His nature. At least I *thought* it was. He had spoken in solemn tones for most of our walk-through, even though He smiled often. But laugh, no. Yet Jesus began laughing out loud, long and hard. *Was He laughing at me?*

I wondered why artists through the years have always pictured Jesus with a Mona Lisa expression. Were they too awed with His divinity to express His humanity? The only time I ever remembered seeing a portrayal of a genuine, happy, laughing Jesus was at a production of *The Promise*. During one scene, the character playing Jesus locked arms with a group of children and adults at a special celebration and danced together in a circle of joyous laughter.

Laughter is a tranquilizer with no side effects.

ANONYMOUS

"Medicine for the soul," Jesus replied matter of factly.

"Medicine. . . ?"

Of course. A joyful heart. . .laughter. . . good medicine (Proverbs 17:22). Was Jesus telling me to lighten up? But hadn't He said to be my natural—which was *serious*—self? *Writing* humor was one thing. But how could an Elizabeth Barrett Browning kind of girl splash her home with colorful laughter?

I had entertained the same question as a Christian writer. Sherwood Wirt once asked C. S. Lewis, "Should Christian writers, then, in your opinion, attempt to be funny?"

Lewis replied, "Some people write heavily, some write lightly. I prefer the light approach because I believe there is a great deal of false reverence about. There is too much solemnity and intensity in dealing with sacred matters; too much speaking in holy tones."[IV]

At a circus, when the lions attack the tamer, the trapeze

artist plunges to the ground, or the cannon misfires, the circus master immediately sends in the clowns to distract the audience and brighten the scene. Surely God could also "send in the clowns" to produce their magical laughter and lighten up my home.

Someone has said, "Laughter is the cheapest luxury that man has. It stirs up the blood, expands the chest, electrifies the nerves, clears away the cobwebs from the brain, and gives the whole system a cleansing rehabilitation."[v] The laughter would come as I learned, like the clowns, to laugh at myself or *with* others, but not *at* others. I soon discovered that it wasn't as hard as I thought.

I tried laughing my way through some of those no-fail jokes in *Reader's Digest*. Once in awhile I'd try to pull one out and share it at the kitchen table. Whoops! Not my style at all. Like that train without a caboose, I'd forget the punch line every time.

But I began to notice something. Humor lay all around me. I just hadn't been looking hard enough:

*In a veterinarian's waiting room: "Be back in five
    minutes. Sit! Stay!"*
*In a restaurant window: "Don't stand there and be
    hungry, come in and get fed up."*
*Inside a bowling alley: "Please be quiet. We need to
    hear a pin drop."*
*On a plumber's truck: "A flush is better than a full
    house."*
On a fence: "Salesmen welcome. Dog food is expensive."
On a maternity room door: "Push, Push, Push."

And it seemed like much of my own humor was accidental. Whenever I travel, I always tell God I'm available if He wants to speak to someone through me. I was trying to start a conversation with a young man sitting beside me on a plane recently. Just as he had settled comfortably into his seat, I asked innocently, "So. Are you traveling for fun or pleasure?"

He slowly turned and looked at me, somewhat amused. "For fun or pleasure?" he repeated.

Did this guy not hear me? "Yes, for fun or. . ." Voila. I never know when my accidental humor is going to kick in.

Laughter is good for the soul. So if you haven't laughed out loud today, go ahead. Release all those happy little hormones. Your body doesn't know the difference between a fake and a real laugh! Maybe you've just been waiting for someone to give you permission to laugh. So here it is. You *can* have fun. Time yourself. Laugh out loud for at least one minute. Now, don't you feel better?

⁓

Larry and I found early on we would have to work at having fun in our marriage. Of course, some of the time, my natural bloopers gave us laughing material. Other times we had to stretch to take one couple's advice: "A giggle a day keeps the therapist away." It was one of those days that led us to the spitting contest.

One day on our back patio, Larry and I gradually moved from shooting the breeze to spitting in the breeze. For some reason I can't remember, one of us spit. Then the other spat. . . spit. . .launched it out there. That's all it took for the "I-can-spit-farther-than-you-can-spit" contest to get underway. By the time we finished, the lawn received a good sprinkling and our stomachs ached from the waves of laughter.

Humor even landed in our mailbox at times. A shocking blooper turned into a good chuckle when my husband and I received a copy of the publicity sheet on the marriage book we wrote several years ago: *Marriage Toners, Weekly Exercises to Strengthen Your Relationship*. In bold print below the title of our book were the following words:

"Here are 52 ways for couples to *sexercise* their way to a fit, healthy relationship." (*Sexercise* should have been *exercise*.)

> *It's a grand person indeed who can laugh at himself with others and enjoy it as much as they do.*
>
> ANONYMOUS

We immediately called our editors. A definite attention-getter, but what were they thinking? Fortunately, they had already discovered their mistake and retrieved several copies sent out in error to some counselors' offices.

Not only does a cheerful heart mean learning to laugh, but it also means creating special moments of pleasure throughout the day. What woman doesn't need a few carefree minutes to call her own, whether in the boardroom or in the backyard? Suzanne Brogger calls them "pleasure stations."

As I thought about my schedule, I realized that I had established some pleasure stations of my own. They were the very things I had been savoring: quiet moments with the Lord, journaling in my backyard hammock, spending time talking to my husband, reading fifteen minutes of a good book, enjoying a cup of French vanilla coffee, steaming in a hot bath, shopping with my grown daughters, or doing lunch with a good friend. No-pressure, guilt-free, motivating moments that we plan for during the day—or even fall into spontaneously.

How long since you had fifteen minutes to call your own, when jelly and peanut butter fingers weren't pulling on your skirt? When your boss wasn't demanding another report at closing time? When you closed your eyes for precious moments alone with your Maker?

Even in the press of the crowd, Jesus escaped. Vanished. On purpose. Sometimes for only a short time. But He stepped in the boat and disappeared or walked up a mountain to pray. Yet He never neglected His calling to heal, to encourage, or to save. He operated in perfect balance.

Create your own pleasure stations—no matter where you are—no matter how crazy and hectic your life is. Take time to celebrate the penny-rich moments of your life. Don't let the tyranny of the urgent destroy the joy of your journey.

The apostle Paul even found joyful experiences in prison. Remembering became an important exercise for him as he wrote letters to his friends back in former churches. Letter writing? Who does that anymore? Today E-mail or a quick phone call has replaced that once pleasurable activity—if pleasurable only to the reader. Some might think, "What a waste of time!" But to a man imprisoned in early retirement, writing letters was a lifeline. And we are the beneficiaries of Paul's joyful letters—journeys of the mind and heart as he retraced the steps from his missionary days, taught lessons he had learned, and shared love through the written page. He could have chosen to sit in his dark cell and complain: "I am here in this dank, smelly prison. The rats are running loose. Some may even be rabid. The chains on my feet hurt, and I never get enough sleep. Every time the jailer jerks, I wake up. Few friends visit me. I'm doomed to die. I'm counting the days until they drag me out and kill me. Oh, woe is me. I never get to eat anything but stale bread and water. This pen leaks; I can't see very well. And I'm getting older by the minute."

Strangely enough, Paul not only found pleasure writing letters (and praying with joy for the people he was writing to (Philippians 1:3–4), he even sang. And his joy was contagious. Earlier in his ministry, when his enemies threw him in prison, Paul and his cellmate Silas began singing and praising God. An earthquake shook the walls; their chains fell off; and Paul joyfully thanked God for witnessing a miracle. The jailer, awestruck with fear and reverence for Paul's God, immediately cried out for salvation. He and his entire household caught the joy of Paul's spirit that day—and their whole destiny changed.

> *Some people complain because God puts thorns on roses, while others praise God for putting roses among the thorns.*
>
> ANONYMOUS

⟿

Personal refreshment contributes to a joyful outlook. And others love to be around happy people. The Bible uses the word *joy* or a derivative of that word at least two hundred times (not counting words like *rejoice* or *happy*). Billy Sunday once said, "If you have no joy in your religion, there's a leak in your Christianity somewhere."

Perhaps Jesus would add, "If you have no *color* in your house, you have no real home." The heart that is joyful is a heart in love with Jesus and those around it. Like Esther Burroughs says, we are to "splash others with living water." Splashes of colorful joy that well up inside us and spill out not only bring refreshment to others, but to ourselves as well.

As Jesus walked through, filling my heart and home with His presence, I discovered all those splashes of colorful joy flowed from a living fountain. Yes, I needed laughter, refreshment, and lighter, pleasant moments. But I could only experience a true, joyful journey when I drank from that Fountain of Life daily.

Master Designer Secret

**"I've told you these things
for a purpose:
that my joy might
be your joy."**

JOHN 15:11 THE MESSAGE

Heart Check

Is there a leak anywhere in your Christianity?

Loving Touches

COLOR-CODED PLEASURE STATIONS

- Green: Spend some time alone with God—prayer, Bible study, meditation.
- Red: Do something you enjoy.
- Burgundy: Do something for someone else—a family member, neighbor, friend, or stranger.
- Blue: Do something that is necessary (not my favorite, but good for me).
- Orange: Do a physical exercise—walking, aerobics, jogging, weight training.
- Brown: Do a mental exercise—reading, writing, journaling.
- Pink: Learn something new—college textbook, magazine, newspaper.
- Purple: Laugh out loud.
- Yellow: Record a blessing—give thanks, writing down if possible.

A Forgiving Place

*Blessed is the home
that never forgets
how to forgive.*

Fill the Candy Jar

Mom, Jared won't leave me alone! I've tried everything I know. But he keeps pestering me, pulling my hair, hitting me. . .what can I do?"

I had been praying about my daughter Jennifer's problem—and for Jared. But so far, God hadn't given me any divine revelations. I was ready to suggest we ask her second-grade teacher to move Jennifer—or Jared—to another seat in the classroom, when a foreign thought occurred to me. Or maybe I should say a *divine* thought. Hadn't I read repeatedly, "Do unto others as you would have them do unto you?" And to be glad "when people insult you?" *Hmmm. Not exactly what I'd do,* I mused. *Reading* what one should do and actually *doing* it were two different things.

There must be another way besides forcibly removing this kid. Of course, I thought. *Jelly beans.*

That week as I shopped at the grocery store, I reached in the gourmet candy bin and scooped out a sack full of multi-flavored, miniature jelly beans. *What kid could resist a handful of jelly beans?*

A few days later, Jared struck again. My daughter returned from school with her usual complaints about her classmate's behavior. "I have just the thing," I replied cheerfully. And I pulled out the sweet bribes from the kitchen pantry.

"Jelly beans? What are these for, Mom?"

"The next time Jared pulls your hair or talks ugly to you, you are going to 'bless' him with jelly beans."

My daughter spit out her next words as if to avoid choking on a sour lemon ball. "Mom, are you crazy? If I give Jared candy every time he does something bad, don't you think it will. . . you know. . .encourage him to keep on pestering me?"

I insisted we try it on faith and see what God would do.

A week later, my daughter walked in the door beaming like the summer sun. "Mom, are you going to the store again anytime soon?"

"Probably, why?"

"Well, Jared said he especially likes the raspberry ones. Mom, he has been so nice to me this week. It worked! It really worked!"

I still remember that incident years ago, but unfortunately I often forgot that principle in my own life—causing me to miss many opportunities to "bless" my enemies.

Forgiveness affirms others with the same grace that God gives to us.

I'm sure there were even times when I questioned the Lord, like the disciples, "Lord, how many times should I forgive someone? Seven times?" A valid, religious answer, and certainly fair according to law.

But Jesus, with wisdom and gentleness answered, "No, seventy times seven."

It wasn't the only time Jesus taught His simple lessons on forgiveness. In Luke 7, Jesus dined in the home of a Pharisee, and a woman with a sinful past approached Him and knelt at Jesus' feet. Her own salty tears mingled with an expensive vial of perfume as she washed the feet of her newfound Master and Friend. Smothering His feet with grateful kisses, she then dried them with her long hair.

The Pharisees criticized Jesus for letting a *sinner* do this—much less a *woman* with her reputation. Yet Jesus seized the opportunity to create a visual word picture and taught an important lesson. Two men owed a debt to a banker—one, five hundred denari, well over a year's salary. The other owed a mere fifty denari, almost two months' wages. The moneylender forgave both debts.

"Which man loved the banker more?" asked Jesus.

The answer was obvious. "The one who had the bigger debt canceled."

Jesus then applauded the woman's actions and reprimanded the Pharisees for their legalistic thinking. "See what this woman has done?" Jesus continued. "You gave me no water for my feet. You did not greet me with a kiss; you did not anoint my head with oil" (traditional hospitality customs extended to guests). "But this woman wet my feet with her tears and dried them with her hair. She has poured fragrant perfume on my feet and has not stopped kissing them," He said. "Her many sins have been forgiven—for she loved much. But he who has been forgiven little loves little."

Then turning to the woman still trembling at His feet, He

wrapped up His precious gift of forgiveness, like a sack full of jelly beans, and handed it to her. "Your sins are forgiven," He said gently. The Pharisees couldn't understand, but the woman received Jesus' gift with gratitude (Luke 7:36–50, with author's paraphrase).

Through the years I've handled the big offenses pretty well. Although some took more time—and jelly beans—with God's help, I have forgiven the perpetrators. It's those little things that sometimes make me forget my divine roots for the moment. Like the time a few years ago when my mom and daughter were visiting me. We were circling the parking lot at our local mall like buzzards, waiting to grab an empty parking space. I was hot, tired, and eager to get on with my business. Finally, I spotted an empty slot and signaled to turn left. I was determined to snatch that space.

About that time a young man on a motorcycle zoomed past me from the other direction—and skidded right into that empty parking space—*my* spot! I'm still not sure what got into me (neither did my mom or daughter), because I've never done anything like it before or since.

No, I didn't run him over or even give him a gentle push. But as I approached the spot where his motorcycle had screeched to a stop, I slowed and rolled down the window. Ignoring the protests of my mom and daughter, I gave the cyclist not a verbal blessing, but a boisterous tongue-lashing.

"Excuse me! Uh, excuse me! Thank you for taking my parking place. I really appreciate that!" I yelled. "That was so thoughtful of you to wait until I could pull in." I continued with a few more choice, sarcastic sentences and finally stopped at the insistence of both passengers in the car. Red-faced from embarrassment and anger, I drove away and immediately stuttered an apology, with an "I-don't-know-what-got-into-me" excuse. *And in front of my own mother and daughter,* I thought.

⎯◌⎯

As Jesus looked around the room, He asked, "Have you been to the candy store lately?"

Maybe that's why recently I decided my grandfather's old gallon peanut jar needed a refill—not of peanuts—but jelly beans. So, now on my dining room buffet sits that old peanut jar—filled with multicolored capsules of forgiveness—a visual reminder that when I bless someone who has mistreated me, I actually invoke God's blessing in the process—to my enemy and to me.

Today, in a society where guns have replaced jelly beans, even in elementary schools, our children may become the innocent targets of another's rage and mounting frustration. Revenge, we think, is sweeter than a jar full of candy. At one time or another, we will have the opportunity to test Jesus' words. We can retaliate or sue. Or we can channel our voices—and our actions—where they can do the most good. To say we need divine help is an understatement.

When we bless someone, we are deciding that he or she is of high value.

GARY SMALLEY and JOHN TRENT, PH.D., *The Blessing*

Offering a sack of jelly beans to someone who has hurt us is neither popular nor reasonable. But in God's upside-down theology, perhaps the things that make the least sense are often the most appropriate actions.

Jesus is teaching me that the simple gift of forgiveness—and blessing—is a lot cheaper than the costly price of a sour apple ball of bitterness. After all He has done for us, can we do any less?

Master Designer Secret

*Do not repay evil with evil
or insult with insult,
but with blessing,
because to this you were called
so that you may
inherit a blessing.*

1 PETER 3:9 NIV

Heart Check

Is there anyone you need to forgive today?

WHAT I'VE LEARNED ABOUT FORGIVENESS

- Forgiveness is a process. Acknowledge the hurt. (Psalm 31:9–10, 32:3–4)
- Forgiveness is divine. Only God can forgive through us. (Ephesians 4:32)
- Forgiveness is an act of the will. We must choose to forgive. (Genesis 37–45)
- Forgiveness is a gift we give, often undeserved. (Hosea 1–3)
- Forgiveness hastens the healing process emotionally, physically, and spiritually. (Psalm 32, 51)
- Forgiveness deepens our capacity to love when we realize the debt owed and the price paid. (Luke 7:47)
- Forgiveness often requires help to release the hurt. (Galatians 6:2; James 5:16)
- Forgiveness makes us a partner in God's reconciliation process and often helps restore the offender. (2 Corinthians 5:18; Luke 15)
- Forgiveness serves the enemy as God brings opportunity. (1 Samuel 24–26; Matthew 5:44)

A Happy Place

Love is a song,
an indelible mark—
an unforgettable melody
written on the heart.

Line the Walls with Music

Before we left our dining room, I noticed Jesus scanning the room. Here was our gathering place for favorite music and familiar memories. On the walls hung two pictures representing the delight of our lives: two bridal collages of our beautiful daughters. A piano sits directly underneath—symbolizing the music of our lives.

Jesus spoke again, pointedly as usual. "Can you still hear the music?"

I didn't know what to say. For several years, pictures, candles, and poetry books have occupied every inch of the mahogany. On the one hand, keeping the lid closed means the ivory keys never get dusty, but it also means they never ring with sweet melodies.

I'm not sure why I reduced this old friend of mine to a mere acquaintance. Perhaps when my children grew up, the music died down. Or maybe because writing took precedence, my fingers chose a keyboard not of ivory, but of hard plastic.

I remember when the song of my life first began—as

Even the deaf ear can hear the melody if it is in tune with the Great Musician.

chubby fingers reached up to touch the music of my mother's heart. I loved to watch her fingers fly over those ivory keys. Then as soon as my feet could touch the floor at the piano bench, she began teaching me the basics. Later she wisely turned me over to other musicians, where my growing, nimble fingers learned to dance lively rhythms. For about ten years the lessons continued. And then, because I wanted an easier route—at least one that did not require memorization for those petrifying recitals—I switched to organ. And then the lessons stopped.

College called, then marriage, and I left my piano behind. But the music never stopped. In fact, maybe that's when the real music of my life began. Suddenly there were no programmed notes to practice, no crowds to applaud at recitals, and no instrument to play—except to accompany church congregations with hearty strains of "Amazing Grace" or "What a Friend We Have in Jesus." You rarely forget how to play the piano. Although skills turn rusty, as long as fingers can move, they can still fly and make music for the soul.

As a young mother in my twenties, I remember standing at the kitchen window one day asking God to fill my heart with a song that would not end. A melody that would linger long after the notes had hushed. Not a masterpiece, not a classic, but a simple melody that would continue through all of the major and minor notes of life. A song that could put a smile on the heart even when all known instruments of joy were silent.

Soon after that, we discovered Colorado as a family. The Rocky Mountain grandeur, the cool mountain streams, and early morning sunrises took my breath away and literally made me break out in spontaneous melody: "The hills are alive with the sound of music!" And they were. I found that out one morning as we stayed with our friends Chet and Millie at their Colorado cabin.

Many summers, in the early mornings, I would steal away to the river just below their cabin. With the orange sun peeking over the blue horizon and a chorus of aspens whistling in rhythm to the rippling waters, I would sit spellbound and just listen. No keyboard could capture this melody, for it was the music of the soul.

As I poured over the pages of familiar Scriptures, it was as if notes began to dance on the page by an invisible hand. I had never had such a feeling of awe, of amazement, of gratitude. An inaudible voice seemed to whisper, "Come—and the music will begin." Each time I would come, thirsty, eager to drink of God's life-giving water, and anxious to hear the promised melodies.

And then I heard them. *Of course,* I thought. *How simple.* Weaving together some basic notes from my childhood storehouse, I began to sing the songs He gave me. Most of the words were not original with me. His words—Scripture— sung back to Him in new melodies. What a wonderful way to remember His own letters to me!

In the months and years that followed, while the children attended school, I found myself lingering more and more in the mornings at our makeshift desk back home. But this time, with pen in hand, I wrote furiously, recording new words,

> *"If they keep quiet, the stones will cry out."*
>
> · LUKE 19:40 NIV

pictures of joy in the morning, cries for hope in the darkness, melodies that freed my spirit—just like my experiences on those crisp, cool, Colorado mornings. On some days, an inner voice chided me, "Why are you wasting so much time?" Then I'd look at the clock, think of the fresh mound of chores and laundry waiting, and pack away my songs.

That's when I remembered again that sinful woman's gift—the expensive vial of perfume poured out on the feet of Jesus. Wasteful? Perhaps. But not to Jesus. You see, each one of us has a song in our hearts just waiting for a recital. It doesn't matter if anyone ever hears it or not. Some songs are given just for the ears of you and your Lover. Like Solomon and his bride, we abandon ourselves to the very One who can make the music sweet—the One who writes the melody for us—so that we can sing it back to Him.

My children learned to play their simple melodies and make beautiful music as blithe fingers glided over those smooth, ivory keys. And I played, too—for church, for myself—and yes, for the Lover of my soul. Sometimes I sang my songs to others; many more lie inside a folder in my file cabinet. A waste of time? I think not. I still sing His song regularly, alongside a group of others in my church choir. It dances in my smile—and sometimes in my fingers when I sign a song to Him in sign language.

Growing up, all three of us kids discovered we had musical talent, but only my brother kept playing regularly.

My sister and I chose to pursue other fields. As a teacher/counselor through the years, she has perfected the art of creating word gifts for the hearts of children—musical, encouraging apples of gold for hungry hearts.

At any given moment, my mom or brother can sit down at the piano and immediately fill the house with sweet melody. Fingers fly from memory and repetition. Mother still plays songs she learned as a girl, flawlessly, without music. She says the exercise keeps her fingers nimble. My brother is a natural composer and arranger whose livelihood nevertheless comes as a computer programmer and analyst. I suspect he plays and sings to keep a song alive in his heart—and because, like me, with creating word pictures, you cannot escape the magnetism of the mysterious melody in our spirits. Once awakened, beauty will not be silent. Never.

God answered my wistful prayer years ago as I stood by that kitchen window. Years later in the blackness of my soul, when depression stalked unmercifully; when another tried to steal the shreds of my dignity; when illness knocked repeatedly; when prayers went unanswered or on hold; when death carried away part of my heart—even through it all, the song He gave me has never died. He stirred up that melody I had heard as a young child. He heard the yearnings of a young mother eager to please. And God has kept His song alive.

⟡

Walking beside my Master Designer, I've been amazed at His discernment, at how quickly He cuts through the heart of a problem and bares the interior of the soul. A few words carefully placed, like a surgeon's sharp instrument, and my defenses bleed away.

Put your hope in God, for I will yet praise him, my Savior and my God.

PSALM 42:5 NIV

Could I still hear the music? I keep praise tapes playing often in my home—always at mealtime and several times throughout the day. Of course I could hear the music. It was woof and warp, the fiber of my being.

I looked at Jesus. *There He goes, reading my thoughts.* The question popped up again.

Could I really still hear the music? I had to find out.

So I returned to the place where I first heard the mysterious melodies almost twenty-five years ago. Eight years had passed since we had basked in the cool mountain air of Colorado. And for almost eight years, maybe more, the ivory keys in my home remained mostly silent.

After a brief stay in Colorado Springs, my husband and I headed toward southwestern Colorado in our rented car. The pines grew taller and the mountains grew larger, it seemed, with every mile. Ever since our first visit to this magnificent vacation state, I had made the same statement: "When we cross the state line into Colorado, something in me just comes alive, and my spirit is set free."

Each time I felt like laughing, playing, crying, praying, shouting, and dancing before the Lord—all at the same time.

But now I grew quieter as I listened. Like an orchestra

leader, I tapped my finger on the window as if to call nature's instruments to attention. The music was about to begin. I could feel it in my spirit. Several hours later, we drove up to the homespun cabin of our friends.

I could hardly wait to rise early the next morning. With Bible, notebook, and pen in hand, I wrapped up in a sweater to face the morning chill and tiptoed out the cabin door. On the front porch bench, with hot tea in hand and a quilt snuggled about her shoulders, sat Millie.

"Come, join me," she said. It had, after all, been years since we had shared a cup of fellowship together.

I sat for a moment, fidgeting. But I kept glancing toward the river. Sensing my uncertainty, Millie said, "It's okay if you want to be alone."

"Well, I uhm. . .sort of. . .wanted to go. . .down to the river," I stuttered.

I hated to abandon my hostess and friend, but I was on a mission. So I headed toward the water. I spotted a large stone a few yards away, sat down, took a deep breath, opened my Bible, closed my eyes, and. . .listened. There they were—the familiar sounds of trickling water, the whistling of the aspens in the wind, and nature's winged chorus chirping their approval to this serene setting. I opened my eyes and glanced down the river. A lone fisherman, casting his lure upon the water in rapid succession, waited expectantly for a trout to bite. Music to his ears.

And as I opened to the Psalms, I, too, like the psalmist David, waited, casting my expectations before the Lord. How many times had David sat beside the still waters, listening to his Good Shepherd's voice, composing these melodies to the

King. I thought of Jesus and how so much of His ministry took place around water: the calling of His fishermen disciples, the teaching and feeding of the multitudes, stilling the stormy Galilean waters. And often, the glassy sea became a bridge of refuge as He escaped from the press of the crowd and sought time with His beloved Father.

> *Let the word of Christ dwell in you richly. . . as you sing psalms, hymns and spiritual songs with gratitude in your hearts to God.*
>
> COLOSSIANS 3:16 NIV

There it was again. That nagging question. *Could I still hear the music?* I chose a less familiar psalm and began to read silently.

And then like a whisper, a still, small voice grew louder as the notes began to dance in my head. A phrase, then a few notes, a prayer, a hum. Soon a full-scale melody escaped my lips in quiet, hushed tones—so softly only the Lord and I could hear. But it was there. The music was there. *Yes!* It was short. But like the "Jesus People" of the seventies, whose bodies swayed and souls stirred with Scripture songs in our church youth groups, I simply took a single verse of Scripture and began humming a melody. God did the rest. My compositions would never top the charts, but hopefully they would tap the heart of God as I sang back the praises David so faithfully recorded so many years ago.

Reluctantly, we returned home several days later, leaving our friends and my beloved musical setting behind.

I've been thinking a lot lately about that closed keyboard in my dining room. Life has a way of stilling the music at times or of making us think we're too deaf to ever hear it again. If I could still hear the music in Colorado, why not here?

So not long ago I headed out to my backyard refuge. The only water sounds I heard there were the neighbor's sprinkler or the birds wallowing in my bird bath. Larry wanted to place a large boulder in the garden for my birthday to symbolize my beloved mountains, but the cost and carry was a little prohibitive for the time being. *Perhaps a fountain might help*, I thought, plotting next year's birthday wish.

As I settled into my hammock, the only whistling I heard were the preschoolers' voices down the street, although on windy days, the trees in my backyard can compose a pretty decent melody.

I wonder. Can I still hear the music—here? I had lingered on the porch many times with Bible in hand. But how long had it been since I had heard a new melody? Was I playing the same old tune? Or worse still, had I silenced the music through neglect or slothfulness? So I took out my Bible and opened to Psalms. Once again, I closed my eyes, breathed a prayer, and asked God for the music to begin.

At first I heard nothing but nature's distractions—a fussy squirrel, a noisy bluejay, the sound of car horns in the distance. But as Jesus silenced my heart and stirred my longings, it was unmistakable. Only a few scattered notes at first. Then more. I looked up, drinking in with delight as heaven played its harmony with my crude efforts. That's when I discovered the secret. The one my Master Designer had been trying to tell me.

Perhaps you've been thinking throughout this chapter, *Oh brother! What a romantic you are! Get real. The music stopped in our household three weeks after we said, "I do." Peanut butter keeps all our ivory keys stuck together, and the house never gets quiet enough to hear my own voice over my teenager's CD—much less some "illusive" melody. I live in the real world, not in some writer's paradise. As far as vacations go? Mountains and rivers, and all that stuff? The mountainous piles of kids' laundry and the gurgling sounds of my washing machine draining are the closest I ever get to that. Of course there is some music—the kind I make when someone cuts me off on the freeway in 7:00 A.M. work traffic.*

Still another may say, *Of course you can still hear the music. You still have YOUR husband. You still have YOUR kids. Oh, I still hear the music, all right. But the melody sounds more like a funeral dirge for me.*

Music is all around us— if we will but take time to listen.

You're right, of course. Except for one thing. The secret. Music does not just whisper through the mountain forest or peaceful rivers. It will stream behind the raging rapids and burst through a splitting earthquake. Melodies are not locked inside romantic hideaways or tucked away in some tragic, forgotten corner. It does not take an orchestra to raise a heavenly symphony. It only takes one listener. Because, you see, music is in the ears of the beholder. And in the heart of the Lover.

Maybe it's time to move the pictures and dusty photographs and let the keys live again. The songs dance on the page and the computer in a different form now, but once in awhile, I ache to give the ivories a chance to laugh and smile again— if only for Him, and maybe for me.

*At night his song is with me—
a prayer to the God of my life.*

PSALM 42:8 NIV

Has anything silenced the music of your heart?

Loving Touches

MY SIMPLE SONG

*I've heard that there is work to do in heaven;
And if that's true, I know what I would do:
I'd love to write the songs they sing in heaven;*

I'd love to make a melody for You.
I'd sing, Father, Abba, Father,
You are all I ever hoped you'd be.
I'd say Jesus, precious Jesus;
You are Life and everything to me.
Lily of the Valley, You're the Fairest of Ten Thousand,
You're the Bright and Morning Star of all my days;
Jesus, precious Jesus,
For You alone, my heart will give You praise.

An Accessible Place

The beauty of the house is order;
The blessing of the house
is contentment;
The glory of the house is hospitality;
The crown of the house is godliness.

<small>Fireplace Motto</small>

Maintain a Sense of Order

As we turned the corner, I was hoping Jesus would not notice the closed door in my hallway. I know what you're thinking. *Rebecca, You have one of THOSE rooms. The kind Robert Munger talked about in his classic booklet "My Heart—Christ's Home."*

But it's not like that. Not exactly. Years ago, Christ had cleaned out my "junk" room, the secret closet, the place we all avoid taking Jesus when He first comes to visit our homes. He and I had no secrets anymore. Then why did I want Him to avoid this room? This was my dreaming room—my office—the place where He helped me create works of heart that I hoped would make a difference for His kingdom.

Remember those boxes of stuff I told you we moved—twice? And the bulging attic where most of it found a home? Although we had packed away most of the contents of the boxes, a few stragglers remained in the garage. I had promised to go through them and either sell or give away the remaining items. But weeks had passed (or was it months?), and those boxes still sat untouched, an obvious eyesore in my husband's pristine garage. I needed time to sort through the good, the bad, and the ugly.

Larry reminded me a few times of my promise, but one day he emphasized it with more emotion. Later that week, God convicted me that maybe I had forgotten the word *submissive,* so I decided here was a good place to start. *I'll surprise him and load up these suckers. Sell the antiques, and even make a little money.* But it didn't work out that way.

I loaded up the boxes, hung up my clothes for the resale shop, and headed out. But no one wanted my goods. The clothes were the wrong season. And what did that sales clerk mean when she said, "Try the vintage shop?" My clothes were in excellent shape for ten years old. Hardly worn. Maybe that's why I had never tried to sell clothes before at a resale store. I always ended up donating them in the hopes someone would think them still fashionable. Even the antique dealer refused my genuine antiques. They were at least thirty years old, if not more!

Discouraged and angry, I sold one huge picture for only five dollars and returned home with full boxes. I started to unpack the car, but then a still, small voice seemed to be speaking. *What about your promise?* So I jumped back in the car, slammed the door, and drove off. *I'll show Larry I can be submissive.* I pulled up at the Salvation Army and unloaded every box and every stitch of clothing. I didn't even flinch when the clerk accidentally broke one of my "antique" vases.

I pulled into the driveway at home, got out, and slammed the car door. *There! I hope he's happy. I submitted!* The boxes were gone. But something else sinister was still lurking nearby.

I kept my deed a secret until a few days later, when Larry

noticed the boxes were gone. I unfolded my story, but somehow the submissive part didn't seem as obvious to him as it did to me. Later on, I went to the garage to find something and looked around at the new space I had created. A strange sense of satisfaction—real fulfillment—flooded me. It felt good to remove that clutter. Like a burden gone.

"I'm so sorry," I whispered to God, like a child caught in the act of disobedience. And then I repeated the words to Larry.

Organization—or the lack of it—had been a hot button for most of our married life. "You don't understand!" I'd plead. "I don't know *how* to organize things! Easy for you. What takes you fifteen minutes to organize takes me two weeks. And then it's back like it was!"

Finally, I guess Larry gave up or accepted me like I was, because he ceased to remind me of those areas anymore.

Love makes up for practically anything.

1 PETER 4:8
THE MESSAGE

He just loved me, messes and all. I relegated most of my piles to one room and declared it "My Office, My Mess, My Business"—and kept the door closed. I reminded him often of why he married me—for my spontaneity, determination, and free spirit. And I reminded him often why I married him—to keep me organized, balanced, and focused.

Acceptance does strange things to a person. I actually got tired of the clutter in my office closet. Tired of looking for "H" files under "B" and a newspaper clipping buried under my filing system on the floor. "Help me!" I begged Larry. "I don't know where to start!" Somehow on paper I managed to create an orderly concert. But in other areas, my methods were more like the orchestra's warm-up.

"Try taking all the stuff out of your closet and putting it in the garage," Larry suggested. "Then go through it one box at a time and move it back one box at a time." Sounded like a good plan. So I filled up his clean garage again with boxes of stuff. Larry didn't count on it taking months to accomplish that task. Neither did I. I wanted my workspace cleaned and organized instantly. When it took me one afternoon to sort through only one box, I whined at the lack of creative writing time, and sneaked back into my office for several days. A month later, I tried again.

Finally, I started moving the boxes back into the closet. It looked. . .presentable, but again full. In the meantime, other clutter had accumulated on my floor and desk again. My office reminded me of the demon-possessed man Jesus talked about in Matthew 12. When the demon couldn't find a resting place somewhere else, it rounded up seven demons more wicked than himself and returned to the clean home to set up housekeeping again. It was the maintenance that was so difficult. I was ready to give up.

⸻

"Are you ready?" Jesus whispered. I nodded, and He opened the door. He didn't flinch, chew me out, or try to shame me. "The important things are not accessible," He spoke softly.

Accessible. I didn't like that word. I was a great speller, but those ten letters ruined my chances at winning the state spelling bee years ago in the sixth grade. I had to settle for runner-up in my school. I never even made it to regionals, much less state championships. But I wasn't sure I understood

Accessible: That which can be found without breaking your neck doing so.

Jesus' words. I only knew I was embarrassed for Jesus to see this mess. My reasons for collecting seemed justified. Every news clipping I had saved was material for a new devotional book. The books on the shelf? All helpful tools for Christian growth and improved writing. Each magazine contained good things to glean—possible quotes for future articles. Every scrap of paper—well, I could eliminate some stuff, I guess. Good things. But the best? Were they all really important?

In the final analysis, no matter how many wonderful things I created and no matter how many times I asked Jesus to redesign my heart, if I didn't maintain it, every space would fill up again with unwanted clutter. But I didn't know *how* to maintain it. That was part of my problem. I wanted an instant cleaning, a clean sweep—perfection—never having to worry about cleaning up messes again.

As if reading my thoughts, Jesus reached over and took my hand. Slowly, methodically, He took outdated thoughts and worn excuses and stuffed the wastebasket until it overflowed. He organized the shelves of my closet and straightened the books against the wall. He opened the squeaky filing cabinet and began tossing away unimportant memos and refiled essential letters. Then He turned to my computer.

Oh, no, I thought. I was mortified. Pride didn't want Jesus to see my scores of unorganized and undeleted E-mails. Tasks undone, lives untouched, stuffed away where no one knew. Like the seven thousand sermons I had heard in my lifetime, how many spiritual messages had I filed away, never acting upon their truth? Lots of knowledge. Abundance of facts. But applied truth? Waiting. Still waiting for action. One by one, Jesus read the thoughts of my heart, compressing the most important into separate folders for easy referral and deleting the rest.

When He finished, I looked around at my office. I could not believe the change. I had surrendered, thinking I would just have to live with this mess forever. Maddening choices of what assignments to write took on new clarity. Sherwood Wirt's motto, "Write about Him," defined my new focus. I would retain only the most essential material that met that criteria. Together Jesus and I made a new sign and hung it on the door. "His Room. His Office. His Business."

⁓

Is your heart cluttered with unnecessary junk mail? Do you struggle daily with the imperfections of your flesh? How many times have you tried to organize your messes, only to throw up your hands in failure?

From the beginning, God set an organized plan in motion, including a plan for our failures. He knew sin would clutter our lives, eventually pushing out every shred of space for goodness. But God in His grace and mercy provided a plan. He first spoke of it in Genesis, just after Adam and Eve's fatal deception. The prophet Jeremiah repeated it along with others throughout the Old Testament: "I know the plans I have for you. . .plans to prosper you and not to harm you, plans to give you hope and a future" (Jeremiah 29:11 NIV).

And then came Jesus. The ultimate plan. In perfect

order—God's way—prophecy fulfilled. Someone who would clean up the world's messes in one divine act of selflessness. The only One who could bring order out of chaos.

God is a God of order. But He is also a God of patience.

⁓

This time, I left the door open. As we walked back through the hallway, I realized Jesus would be there to applaud me in my strengths; but He would also hold my hand in times of weakness. No once and for all cleaning. No instant perfection—not in my performance, at least. Only in my position as His acceptable, beloved child. His strength would be sufficient. In my ignorance, He would grant wisdom. He would bring order to my days and motivation from my slackness. He would keep my heart clean as I submitted to Him daily.

Just like He did for Peter, Jesus would take my failures and inadequacies and turn them into something beautiful. And just in case I forgot how He did it, He would fill my file folders full of essential, *accessible* memories—reminders of His faithfulness, goodness, and love.

And what Jesus will do for me, He'll do for you, too. That's an accessible promise.

God was reconciling the world to himself in Christ, not counting men's sins against them.

2 CORINTHIANS 5:19 NIV

Master Designer Secret

But everything should be done in a fitting and orderly way.

1 CORINTHIANS 14:40 NIV

Heart Check

How accessible is your heart?

Loving Touches

RULES OF THE HOUSE

If you open it_____close it
If you get it out_____put it away
If you sleep in it _____make it up
If you drink out of it_____wash it
If you take it off_____hang it up
If you turn it on _____turn it off
If you drop it_____pick it up
If you clip it _____file it
If it hurts _____comfort it
If it cries _____love it

An Intentional Place

Love keeps us close
to the heart of God.

Remember the Basics

No one prepared me for people like Miss Gordy. Not even growing up in a minister's family taught me the skills to deal with that irregular ninety-something woman in our first country church.

Miss Gordy's greeting on Larry's first Sunday, "You're just a kid!" only fueled my fears of inadequacy. Among her many antics, one episode stands out distinctly:

One weekend we were walking downtown ("down-town" being one restaurant, a gas station, and a faded, red-brick post office), when we heard a loud commotion behind us.

"Look out—Oh, Lordy!" someone yelled. "Here comes Miss Gordy!"

We looked up in time to see our local senior daredevil gunning her 1955 Plymouth in reverse down the old highway—straight toward us and the post office. Even having a disabled forward gear couldn't stop Miss

Gordy. We dove for cover and narrowly missed a shower of flying bricks as she backed full speed into the corner of the post office.[VI]

⸺ꗃ

Jesus' next words reminded me of our beginnings as a husband and wife in ministry and of that incident involving the infamous Miss Gordy. "Remember the basics," said Jesus, as we walked through the hallway. A familiar principle of interior decorating: line, balance, color—we had about covered them all in our walk-through. But the way Jesus spoke those words reminded me that basics often meant more—it also meant "beginnings."

I remembered Coach Vince Lombardi's words to his football players at halftime, following an inferior performance one day: "Gentlemen, this is a football." Realizing his players needed some quick motivation, he challenged them to remember, to go back to the basics of the game of football.

> *The secret of success is start from scratch and keep on scratching.*
>
> ANONYMOUS

Larry and I had used both of those illustrations often to explain how we, too, retreated to the beginning of our relationship. Like Miss Gordy, we had to "go backward" in order to "go forward."

I was only thirteen when this six-foot-one, handsome guy in jeans sat beside me one night in church. So what if there were no other seats available in our youth section? I convinced myself Larry picked that seat just so he could discover my alluring charms. A year and a half later, I finally charmed him into asking me for a date (after *I* had asked *him* to two church functions). After my freshman year in college, we said, "I do," and sailed off into our Prince Charming, Cinderella world.

For fifteen years, we managed fairly well—by agreeing to let Larry be right most of the time. But after two children and several years in the ministry, we woke up one day to realize our ideal marriage had taken a wrong turn. Not knowing how to bridge the emotional distance that had crept in, we sought help. The counselor's plan? "Larry and Rebecca, this is a marriage." And he took us backward—all the way back to the beginning of what a relationship should be. Just as no one (not even seminary professors) had really prepared us for the real world of ministry, no one prepared us for the real world of marriage, either.

In Revelation 2, the church at Ephesus was told they had lost their first love for Jesus. We realized we had lost our first love for each other in the same way. Here's the principle that pointed our marriage back in the right direction:

"Remember the height from which you have fallen! Repent [turn around—go back] and do the things you did at first." REVELATION 2:5 NIV

So we did.

We relearned how to talk to each other—to really communicate for understanding. More than the usual seventeen minutes a week of conversation that the average couple spends together talking, we began to set a "check-in" time each day. We worked at carving out a minimum of ten minutes

141

somewhere during that day, where we would sit face-to-face, knee to knee, and share a "State of Our Union" address to each other: "Come on into the living room of my heart. What are you feeling today? What's going on in your life? What needs or pressures are you facing today? What good things are happening? Are there any issues we need to talk about?"

Each Sunday afternoon we spent an hour together in calendar planning and more intensive talking. At first we felt like awkward teens on their first date, but we kept planning intentional sessions, just as if we had scheduled a business appointment. Slowly we relaxed.

Larry and I learned how to listen with "a third ear," where we literally "went fishing" into each other's hearts to catch more understanding. Ever try to concentrate on what the other person is saying without planning a rebuttal of your own? Larry was particularly skilled in "fishing" and drawing a big catch as he would repeat what he *thought* I was trying to say. Many times he helped me to understand my own feelings, when I didn't have a clue myself.

We also tried placing an invisible shield about ourselves and tried to allow the Holy Spirit to deflect any defensiveness on our part and allow us to listen to each other even if the words hurt. "Venting" was permitted and understood in our marriage for the first time, but we worked on eliminating accusations.

Like two old-fashioned sweethearts courting, we started dating again, something we had forgotten to do regularly. In earlier years, we had learned to "abandon" occasionally—every year or two—but unfortunately, when we returned home, life had also returned to normal—he in his work and me in homemaking, parenting, and writing.

Dating reaffirmed those loving feelings, as did intentional gifts and surprises we planned for each other—gifts that said, "I care about you. You are number one in my life. You are special." At first, I felt selfish making "I want" lists, but soon had trouble squeezing my requests onto only two pages.

> *A marriage continues to sizzle when its partners get serious about fanning the flames.*
>
> LARRY AND
> REBECCA JORDAN,
> *Marriage Toners*

Back rubs? Mmmmm. Morning coffee on my bedside table? Yes! As we exchanged lists and purposely affirmed each other daily, whether we felt like it or not, we made two surprising discoveries: (1) We had truly "fallen" in love again, and (2) we could now discuss some hot-button issues that were formerly considered taboo—without resorting to withdrawal, defensiveness, or tears. The consistent love actions, dates, and genuine communication had opened the door to a deeper intimacy.

But I would be less than honest if I did not tell you that the work of marriage is difficult and at times discouraging. We often fall back into old patterns. Keeping that balance takes much prayer and will always be challenging. But a deep commitment to each other and an intentional desire to honor Jesus Christ through our marriage keeps us focused and eager to grow in oneness together even through difficult years. God has been patient with us.

Several years ago we discovered that not only could our

marriage benefit us and our children (they noticed the difference, too), but others, as well.

We had agreed to sell a puppy for our oldest daughter. A young woman answered our ad and bought that cocker spaniel pup. Unfortunately, in the process, I had become attached to that little ball of fur. When I watched that sweet puppy walk out of our lives, I couldn't hold back the tears. Can you believe that? As we watched them go, Larry reached over and gave me a tender, reassuring hug—nothing unusual.

The young lady brought the dog back the next day. Her landlord refused to allow it into the apartment complex. Before she left, she blurted, "Someday, I want a marriage like yours."

"What do you mean?" I asked, puzzled by her statement.

"You know, the way your husband hugged you when I left yesterday. I could tell you love each other by the look in your eyes."

It was a simple observation. But we got the message. People are watching our marriages to see if the light's really on. If the walk matches the talk. If the marriage works. If the vows stick. Before that young lady left, we had the privilege of introducing her to the only true Light we know.

> *Duty makes us do things well, but love makes us do them beautifully.*
>
> ANONYMOUS

———

The basics. Necessary steps to learning anything. Even Leonardo da Vinci learned how to mix colors before he could paint a masterpiece. Surely Chopin mastered basic theory before composing a concerto. Children collect tons of Band-Aids before they learn to walk. And athletes sweat through endless hours of practice before snatching an Olympic gold medal.

Robert Fulghum speaks humorously of the basics all of us are taught as children in kindergarten:

Share everything.
Play fair.
Don't hit people.
Put things back where you found them.
Clean up your own mess.
Don't take things that aren't yours.
Say you're sorry when you hurt somebody.
Wash your hands before you eat.
Flush.
Flush. [I would add this twice. Some kids need a
    double reminder.]
Warm cookies and cold milk are good for you.
Live a balanced life—learn some and think some and
    draw and paint and sing and dance and play and
    work every day some.
Take a nap every afternoon.
When you go out into the world, watch out for traffic,
    hold hands, and stick together.
Be aware of wonder. Remember the little seed in the
    Styrofoam cup: The roots go down and the plant
    goes up and nobody really knows how or why, but
    we are all like that.
Goldfish and hamsters and white mice and even the little
    seed in the Styrofoam cup—they all die. So do we.

*And then remember the Dick-and-Jane books and the
first word you learned—the biggest word of all—
LOOK.[VII]*

God gave ten basic rules in the Ten Commandments, but
all of them can be summed up in these two arching laws:

"Love the Lord your God with all your heart and soul
and mind, and your neighbor as yourself." Pretty basic stuff.
"And I have come to fulfill the law," Jesus said, speaking of
His own death, burial, and resurrection, by which every person is made "lawful," or right with God.

Jesus knew the weakness of our human flesh. After we
had made our vows to Him in a personal relationship, Jesus
knew we would need to brush up on the basics often. That's why
John reminded the church at Ephesus about that basic premise:
"You have left your first love." You've forgotten the basics. Look
where you are at point B. And think back to where you started at
point A. Then start over.

If you want to discover God's plan for your life, you must first read the blueprints.

Like a home run hitter who
slid into home base without touch-
ing first, some of us may need to dust off our knees and return
to first base. Larry and I did. And I knew with Jesus' personal
reminder to me that I needed to revisit that place often. Maybe
that's why every couple needs to take a "Memory Journey" from
time to time. There, we can all revisit the place where our relationships first began. There, we can fan the fires of first love.

There, we can recommit ourselves to the everyday work of marriage—going backward to go forward. If it was true in my marriage, how much more did I need to return continually to the basics of my first love with Jesus?

—⌒—

Has anything or anyone replaced your first love with your mate? How long has it been since you examined your marriage progress in the light of your first vows? Has anything or anyone come between you and your God? Is your relationship with Jesus still sweet and strong?

Evangelist Malcolm Ellis once offered these guidelines about determining Jesus' place in our lives. It may be a good test to see if we have really lost our first love:

- Does anyone's opinion or good pleasure hold more power over you than the Lord's?
- Does anything give you more personal pleasure than being radically right with God?
- Do you think you have to have something other than Jesus to make you happy?
- Do you treat the clear commands of God as if they were suggestions we can debate and decide upon?

If the answer to any of those questions is yes, you're probably not alone.

Would you like to go for a drive with me? Put your seat belt on. The forward gear is stuck. Hang on tight. We'll have to shift it into reverse.

Master Designer Secrets

Remember the day you stood
before the Lord your God.

DEUTERONOMY 4:10 NIV

Heart Check

Have you taken a personal memory journey lately?

Loving Touches

A VOW OF RENEWAL

I, _____, renew my vows to you this day in God's sight, and in the presence of these witnesses. I will love you, cherish you, hold you in high esteem, and be in every way a faithful and intentional husband/wife, regardless of the circumstances, 'til death shall part us. I ask your forgiveness for failures, your patience for shortcomings, and your love to cover my faults. I pledge to make our home a spiritual refuge, a loving retreat, and a welcome place for understanding. I also commit myself to be a woman/man after God's own heart, with the desire to put Him first in my life and in our marriage.

You will be my special treasure, a beautiful gift from God, and I promise to value and nurture you—and our marriage—daily. I will be your faithful friend, your loving companion, and your spiritual partner in serving God together—all the days of our lives. I will love you with a servant spirit, putting your needs above my own. With all my love, with all my life, I make these vows to you today.

A Grace-Full Place

True kindness is never random,
but a purposeful gift
of grace from the heart.

Add Loving Touches

"Are your baskets full?" said Jesus, as we entered the extra bedroom. It was the guest room, still under construction, but prepared with loving touches for the comfort and enjoyment of overnight guests.

His gaze fell to the basket on my guest bed. Inspired by my sister and daughters, I had purchased some special toiletries and gift products to fill what I called my basket of "escentials." Whenever guests visited, I encouraged them to use the goodies as their own. But inevitably after they left, I noticed most of the items sat untouched.

At first, I was disappointed. Didn't they like what I bought? Did they prefer a different fragrance? After all, these were *my* choices. I assumed others would like them, too.

"Well, I brought my own stuff," they'd reply when I asked them later.

Perhaps I should have remembered a lesson I learned years ago: One person's essentials can be another's burdens.

I met Joan one Sunday years ago and rejoiced as she embraced Grace for the first time. Gratefully, like a weary traveler in the desert, Joan invited that beautiful Person to fill her life. She didn't understand everything at the time, but she eagerly began her new commitment. Her story may be a familiar one:

A few weeks after she meets Grace, Joan leaves her toddler with a neighbor and dashes out to do some quick shopping before the other kids return from school. Then she runs into the department store where an aggressive, cosmetic consultant stops her and offers a free facial. Joan agrees. The woman says to snag her husband's affections and stay beautiful, Joan must buy four hundred dollars' worth of cosmetics each month. Every woman *must* take care of herself. Outer beauty is an important frame for our inner radiance. Just look at Queen Esther in the Bible, the woman says. She is passionate.

> *Everyone has the right to express an opinion; however, no one has the right to expect everyone to listen.*
>
> ANONYMOUS

Joan grabs a few products and heads for the dress department, where another sales clerk immediately points her to a wardrobe guaranteed to make her a fulfilled woman. Small cost for great dividends, she says with passion. Only one thousand dollars. The young mother thanks her politely, promises to think about it, and heads out with a twenty-five dollar formfitting bra to wear under her seven-year-old, basic black dress.

As Joan pulls in the driveway, a neighbor from her church approaches her and asks if she could teach a Bible class the following year. They need teachers. It is *so* important. She can't say no. Who will spread the good news if not people like you and me? We must feed people with the Word. She is passionate.

Joan walks in the door and grabs the ringing phone. Her husband, who has been a committed Christian for several years, says they should invite the Smiths over Friday for dinner. They need friends, and hospitality is so important. In fact, what does she think about having guests over every Friday night? They could even start a prayer group in their home to reach their neighborhood. Okay? He'll see her after awhile.

His wife tucks away her purchases and the phone rings again. Each child yells, "Mine!" as Joan wrestles the phone away from sticky fingers. The children's choir director at church is calling to ask if she would help with choir this year. Yes, children are important. Yes, Joan agrees they are the future of our world. She has four of them, all of whom are tugging on her skirt right now. Well, what about singing in the adult choir? Oh, the lady is on that committee, too. Well, yes, she loves to sing, but. . .yes, she knows praise ushers us into the presence of God. The woman is passionate. Yes, well. . .Joan says she'll pray about it.

Joan prepares a light snack for the kids and opens the mail. There, from the church finance committee chairman, is a letter from the "Build We Must" campaign and he is passionate about giving sacrificially. It is her Christian duty. Future generations of believers depend on her gift. Can she stretch and give two hundred dollars a month and every month for five years until the building is paid for? Think of the people saved if she will give her part—people who will then have a place to hear the gospel.

Soon after her husband's arrival, Joan quickly throws on her basic black dress. They grab a quick McDonald's meal and head for church. Following the benediction, the young mother turns to leave and her Sunday school teacher taps her on the shoulder. "Accountability check. How's your quiet time lately?"

Quiet time? What's that? Joan thinks as she smiles.

The new Christian mom goes home, tucks her kids in bed, tries to be passionate as she kisses her husband good night, and then collapses beneath the covers herself. An hour later, Joan wakes up, frantic. She remembers one child she didn't kiss good night. Where was she? Did she leave her at church? Joan races to her daughter's bedroom. She is not there. The living room, kitchen, not there. She runs to the garage, opens the car door. Her daughter is not there. To the backyard, front yard. She looks down the street. There is no sign of her daughter. She runs back in and wakes up her husband. She screams, "Call the police!"

"What's the matter?" he asks through bleary eyes.

Her daughter is missing. She cannot find Grace.

Her husband looks at her dumbfounded. "Honey, you must be dreaming. Come with me."

And he takes her to the next room, where Grace is sleeping soundly. She cannot resist the urge to scoop up Grace, hold her tightly to her chest, and smother her with hugs and kisses.

"It was all a dream?" she asks her husband. She returns Baby Grace to her crib and goes back to bed.

"It was all a dream," she repeats, still trying to convince herself. "The whole day."

Her husband looks at her questioningly.

It was a dream, wasn't it? she thinks as she drifts back to sleep.

———

We cannot quell the hunger in our souls with more work or piety— often what we really need is rest— sweet rest in Jesus.

"Only one thing is essential." I hear those familiar words of Jesus softly penetrating my thoughts again.

As you read that story, with whom did you identify? Have you, like Joan, searched for answers about the Christian walk? Have others given you countless advice on essential Christian disciplines and extended numerous invitations for service?

Those who are seeking answers on how to live their faith can quickly become confused. Each believer may feel passionately about what is most important in God's service. In your quest for answers, you may have asked, "Where do I fit into God's plan?"

Or maybe you plead guilty along with the Christians in 1 Corinthians who insisted, "My gift is better than your gift." Without realizing it, you lost sight of grace for a season and offered to others what you thought were the essentials for being a good Christian.

I must admit, I've probably stood on both sides. As a young seeker, I wanted truth. But in my thirst for knowledge and perfection, I listened more to others than God's Word

> *See to it that no one misses the grace of God.*
>
> HEBREWS 12:15 NIV

and soon joined them in forming the new "Ten Commandments for Christian Service." I spent years swinging on the pendulum until God showed me a new meaning of grace.

Just as we cannot raise carbon copy children, neither does God clone Christians into His kingdom. He wants each of us to grow into His likeness and to serve Him the way He has gifted us. Each discipline and each gift is valuable, but we will not agree on how to prioritize them.

I can be a klutz at times in the kitchen. But I still serve my burnt offerings and basic meals to my family and occasionally someone who is sick (if it won't hinder the recovery). But I love teaching. Even when I do take someone a meal, I may end up trying to teach them a Bible truth. It's my nature.

As a greeting card writer, I can exercise another gift of mine—showing mercy and encouragement to help people feel better emotionally. But you know the kind of cards I enjoy writing most? Those that teach a truth about God. In fact, most of all, I love to teach, encourage, serve, and even pray—through writing. God's commands require obedience, but He allows me the grace to serve Him in the way He has gifted me. The "disciplines" such as Bible study, prayer, and service strengthen my relationship with the Giver of every good and perfect gift—but they are not substitutes *for* the relationship.

There is no excuse for apathy in any area of our lives. No matter what our occupation or area of service to God may be, He tells us to "do all to the glory of God." Each discipline is important to our growth. But neither is there a reason for "gracebusting," a word Chuck Swindoll so aptly coined. When someone expresses the "you-are-not-living-for-God-unless-you-are-ministering-the-way-I-am" philosophy, it may not be passion, but idolatry.

At one Christian Booksellers Convention, I was talking with a prospective editor about some of my book proposals. He asked me a question: "What is your passion?"

I thought of many passions—teaching, gardening, reading, marriage, family. But I answered his question as honestly as I could. "Writing." I am passionate about writing. I love to write.

Later I saw that same editor and amended my statement. "What I am really passionate about is knowing God's heart. I have a passion for God. And I enjoy writing about Him." Stemming from that main passion are many subjects about which I can be excited, but I want them all to center on Him.

It sounded good. Was it true? Time would tell. If my passion replaces the Person, then my passion becomes an idol. Grace is willing to share its viewpoints and its gifts without a one-size-fits-all only mentality. The one "escential" is Christ Himself.

The spiritual gifts and ministries given to us, according to Scripture, are by their very nature and Greek meaning "grace" gifts. Grace allows us to understand and appreciate the value of each person's individuality and keeps our eyes focused on the Servant, not the service, and on the Giver, not the gift.

Joan needed basketsful of understanding and the wise counsel of others to prevent helplessness from consuming her new walk in Christ. Instead, she received a flurry of opinions that left her guilt-ridden and confused. She needed assurance that, in time, God would reveal her personal place in this world to serve Him. Grace replaces the broken record of guilt with a new melody.

> *God's purpose is not to perfect me to make me a trophy in His showcase; He is getting me to the place where He can use me. Let Him do what He wants.*
>
> OSWALD CHAMBERS,
> *My Utmost for His Highest*

Grace. Such a beautiful but misunderstood word. Max Lucado says, "Grace means you don't have to run anymore! It's the truth. Grace means it's finally safe to turn ourselves in."[VIII] God's grace never leaves us. We simply misplace it.

Grace doesn't force itself on others. It is like a mother eagerly prodding her children on the right path, but giving them time to learn. It is Christ Himself who gently ushers Grace into our hearts. And His Grace will never lead us astray. In the words of the old hymn written by John Newton:

> *'Tis grace hath brought me safe thus far,*
> *And grace will lead me home.*

Without Grace, failure has no value. Without Grace, service has no benefit. Without Grace, there is no gift. Without the gift, there is no Giver.

I looked at the basket again on the guest bed. *There is a missing ingredient here,* I thought. And then I remembered the basket in the guest bathroom as well. It was time to fill *all* the baskets with "escentials" that really mattered.

Master Designer Secret

*We have different gifts,
according to the grace given us.*

ROMANS 12:6 NIV

Heart Check

Have you visited the place of grace lately?

Loving Touches

BASKET OF "ESCENTIALS"

Select a large, sturdy basket and tie a colorful bow around the handle.

Then "grace" your gifts by stocking the basket with guest essentials. Purchase small travel sizes and choose from the following items:

toothpaste	mouthwash	bath gel
bath powder	bath sponge	razor
hand cream	shave lotion	shave cream
Tylenol or aspirin	breath mints	candy pieces
shampoo	conditioner	tea bags
coffee	snack crackers	cookies
fragrant candle	current magazines	devotional book
New Testament	guest towels	washcloths

Use your imagination, and ask yourself the question: "If I were staying in a bed and breakfast, what special loving touches would I like to find waiting for me?" If possible, keep a notebook of regular guests' preferences (such as grown children or other relatives).

A Wonder-Full Place

Simple childhood pleasures
are some of God's best treasures.

Child-Proof Your Home

Is the child alive?" asked Jesus before we left the guest bedroom.

His question contained no explanation, no transitional statement. It made no sense. I watched as He stooped down and picked up a dusty, ragged bear from a cluster of four-legged creatures on the floor.

I immediately thought of Jesus' words to me a few months earlier. I was sitting in church on a Sunday night, and my precise prayer that day had been, "Lord, I need to hear from You. Search my heart. Show me anything that needs changing today. I need a personal word from You."

As my mind often does, about halfway through the evening service, my thoughts departed on some flight of fancy. A phrase kept running through my mind. At first I dismissed it and tried to concentrate on the message from the pulpit. But then I remembered my earlier prayer. The phrase was part of a Scripture, but it sounded like a direct command to me: "Put away childish things." Lest you think I'm prone to visions and such things, this was not a usual occurrence.

I immediately felt a mixture of conviction and sorrow. Conviction that maybe God was asking me to give up something in my life. Sorrow that it was something I enjoyed.

The something just happened to be a collection of small, furry creatures.

Cherub-faced dolls and stuffed animal friends had filled the nooks and crannies of my childhood bedroom. As an adult I had stored my collection in containers, determined to sell them someday "when I need the money for the girls' college." But college had come and gone, and most of the familiar toys still sat unsold, collecting dust. Recently, I had pulled a few childhood friends out of storage to liven up my guest bedroom.

I had not added to my collection in a good while. Instead, I moved on to other pursuits and interests. But somehow I joined a popular craze with some of my relatives. The "Beanie Baby bug" bit, and it bit hard. *This is an investment*, I reasoned, as I stood in frenzied lines and made frequent calls: "Do you have any new Beanie Babies?" After a handful of tiring episodes, I shunned the long lines and often purchased either by Internet or through friends.

> *"For where your treasure is, there your heart will be also."*
>
> LUKE 12:34 NIV

I rationalized to my husband: "It's like going fishing for the big one. You never know what you might catch." Early in the hunt, bears emerged as the hot commodity. And after all, the collection *was* a fun connection with relatives as we'd call or E-mail to report on our latest treasures or exchange our rare finds as Christmas gifts.

But the beanie hunts were also time consuming. "It keeps the child alive in me," I'd reason, whenever doubts crept in about the wisdom of my growing collection.

So when I heard those words that Sunday evening, *Put away childish things,* I immediately thought, "Oh no! God means my Beanie Babies!"

I learned my lesson. Others seemed to know when to "hold 'em and fold 'em." I knew only how to hold 'em. When the beanie boom turned to beanie bust, I was left holding the much-devalued beanbags. (Anyone need a nice, mint, furry creature for Christmas?) Unfortunately I entered the beanie rush too late. By the time I started collecting, so had everyone else. I owned not even one rare beanie.

But I soon realized that Jesus' words did not refer to my childish collections. How could I keep the child alive and put away childish things at the same time?

⸻

Jesus loved children. I can still visualize Him surrounded by dimpled preschoolers and school-aged kids, all begging for a coveted place in His lap or a touch from His gentle hand. A mother places her babe into Jesus' arms, and the child is mesmerized by eyes that know how to emit only perfect love.

The disciples didn't understand. "These children are a bother!" they protested "Take them away! Jesus is too busy!" they yelled to the pint-sized admirers and their moms.

But Jesus rebuked the disciples for their shortsightedness

and faulty thinking. Underlining the importance of children, Jesus insisted we keep the child alive in us. "Let the little children come to me, and do not hinder them, for the kingdom of heaven belongs to such as these" (Matthew 19:14 NIV).

A child's footsteps will lead us to the Father's own heart.

In an earlier discussion with His disciples on greatness, Jesus said this about children: "I'm telling you, once and for all, that unless you return to square one and start over like children, you're not even going to get a look at the kingdom, let alone get in. Whoever becomes simple and elemental again, like this child, will rank high in God's kingdom. What's more, when you receive the childlike on my account, it's the same as receiving me" (Matthew 18: 3–5 THE MESSAGE).

So heaven is full of children? Or childlike attitudes? I wondered.

Years later the apostle Paul wrote these guidelines for adult behavior: "When I was a child, I talked like a child, I thought like a child, I reasoned like a child. When I became a man [woman], I put childish ways behind me" (1 Corinthians 13:11 NIV).

I was a little confused. What childish attitudes did Jesus want me to keep alive? And what childish things should I put away?

For a few minutes I tried to remember the sights and smells of childhood—the joys, the fears, the laughter, the tears. Roller skates and tricycles, the innocence of life, hide-and-seek and hopscotch, dress-up, make-believe. Cinnamon pie sticks, Christmas wonder, bloodied knees, and homework pleas. Childhood can be wondrous, scary, fun, or hurtful, depending on our environment, our experiences, and the homes we inherited.

But it was Jesus' opinion I valued at this moment. Suddenly, my Master Designer interrupted my thoughts. "Come with Me," He said. "I'll teach you the difference." So together we sat down and opened His Word. I imagined myself as one of His followers on the Judean hillside, as we walked through Scripture together. For a few moments, Jesus reverted to direct, didactic teaching instead of His usual gentle prodding. Perhaps the tender subject of children moved Him to clarify exactly how He felt. I sat at the feet of the One who had also become my Master Teacher through the years. Our search revealed a dichotomy of truths but also showed me the key to my dilemma. Here is what Jesus taught me:

• *Children are natural imitators.* James Baldwin once said, "Children have never been very good at listening to their elders, but they have never failed to imitate them." Inevitably our parents influence us. Wise adults will keep imitating the positive traits they observed in their parents, but learn from and abandon the hurtful, dysfunctional ones. More than anything, we are to copy our Heavenly Father.

> *Watch what God does, and then you do it, like children who learn proper behavior from their parents. Mostly what God does is love you. Keep company with him and learn a life of love. Observe how Christ loved us. His love was not cautious but extravagant. He didn't love*

in order to get something from us but to give everything of himself to us. Love like that.

EPHESIANS 5:1–2 THE MESSAGE

• *Children need to be nurtured.* An infant's needs are simple: love and nourishment. They are entirely dependent on their parent providers. Yet as a child grows, he learns to demand less and give more. Let Christ continue to nurture you. Keep your dependency on Him, but put away selfish, greedy wants. Reach out to care for others as He cares for you.

"But we were gentle among you, like a mother caring for her little children." 1 THESSALONIANS 2:7 NIV

Children hear the whispers of God's own heart; eagerly they pause and give praise to the Lord.

• *Children are uninhibited in their love and adoration.* They'll sing, "Jesus loves me," in the supermarket without worrying about what people think. They'll throw their arms around you, and in the middle of someone's solemn church prayer, they will unabashedly exclaim, "Mommy, I love you!" But you may also catch those same children in a pinching match with other preschoolers screaming, "Mine!"

Keep spontaneous, God-pleasing, uninhibited praise and worship of the Lord, and show appropriate love affirmations to those around you. Put away unchecked anger and selfish, reactive behaviors that hurt and destroy.

> *When the religious leaders saw the outrageous things he was doing, and heard all the children running and shouting through the Temple, "Hosanna to David's Son!" they were up in arms and took him to task. "Do you hear what these children are saying?"*
>
> *Jesus said, "Yes, I hear them. And haven't you read in God's Word, 'From the mouths of children and babies I'll furnish a place of praise'?"*
>
> MATTHEW 21:15–16, THE MESSAGE

• *Children see and understand things that the wise and intelligent miss.* One day my youngest daughter accidentally spilled a bottle of hair gel. As the gooey mess started oozing down the side of an upholstered chair onto the new carpet, I opened my mouth to protest. But before my words escaped, my other daughter sang out, "Oh, well, Mommy. Praise the Lord, anyway!" Listening to the wisdom of children keeps our eyes open to see divine truths we may otherwise miss. Keep childish eyes, and don't let ladder climbing and college degrees crush the simplicity of life's lessons.

> *At that time Jesus said, "I praise you, Father, Lord of heaven and earth, because you have hidden these things from the wise and learned, and revealed them to little children."*
>
> MATTHEW 11:25 NIV

Keep the humility of childhood that does not claim to know everything, but is eager and teachable. Cling to what is known, but broaden your thinking patterns to embrace new insights, open to change, sorting out what is right and wrong. Put away haughty, proud spirits that refuse to budge.

• *Children need—and crave—blessing.* Perhaps you are still seeking your parents' approval and blessing. Grades never met their expectations; careers didn't equal their criteria; behaviors were never quite right. Recognize that your parents may never know how to give their blessing, but understand it could be because they failed to put away their own childish expectations. They may have substituted things and gifts for time and affirmations. But to them, it spelled love—in the best way they knew how to show it.

Realize that your Heavenly Father has given you His utmost blessing and approval. Desire the Lord's blessing, but put away the fear that He will remove it forever if you make a mistake. Then you will be free to give yourself away as a blessing to others as well. Don't stay around the table when there is work to do in the field.

> *The people brought children to Jesus, hoping he might touch them. . . . But Jesus was irate and let them know it: "Don't push these children away. Don't ever get between them and me." Then gathering the children up in his arms, he laid his hands of blessing on them.*
> MARK 10:13–16 THE MESSAGE

• *Children need warning and instruction.* Don't our mothers still occasionally warn us, "Get enough rest. Are you working too hard? Are you taking your vitamins? Be careful!" It's a good idea to heed the warning and instruction you received as a child *and* as a new believer. Never think you are too old to be warned. The moment we leave the safety of God's protective wings, we move into deadly enemy territory.

I'm not writing all this as a neighborhood scold just to make you feel rotten. I'm writing as a father to you, my children. I love you and want you to grow up well, not spoiled. There are a lot of people around who can't wait to tell you what you've done wrong, but there aren't many fathers willing to take the time and effort to help you grow up.   1 CORINTHIANS 4:14–15 THE MESSAGE

• *Children are innocent to evil.* True, we are born with sin natures that develop with time. But it would be cruel to hit an innocent baby because it cried for food or needed a diaper change. At that stage of their lives, children are not capable of evil. As you grow older, keep a guileless attitude when it comes to determining right and wrong. Put away the tendency to say yes to harmful things.

Look back so that you may be yourself as you really were intended to be— a child of God set free by the healing power of the Holy Spirit.

DAVID A. SEAMANDS,
Putting Away Childish Things

How long before you grow up and use your head—your adult head? It's all right to have a childlike unfamiliarity with evil; a simple no is all that's needed there.

> *But there's far more to saying yes to something. Only mature and well-exercised intelligence can save you from falling into gullibility.*
>
> 1 CORINTHIANS 14:20 THE MESSAGE

• *Children know their identity.* As a child I never questioned who my parents were. They treated me like their child. They loved me as their own. And I saw the birth certificate. Children who are adopted may not feel that same sense of identity until they grasp the reality of what true family means. Wise parents give their adopted children space, time, and love to help them achieve a sense of belonging, especially when they question or challenge that truth.

Even adults may temporarily lose their identity through dysfunctional patterns of fear, comparison, or perfectionism. But when they can grasp the truth that they have been adopted into the family of God, their true identity once again emerges. Keep that childhood identity alive. Your Father loves you totally and unconditionally. Put away rejection. You are God's child! Our faith in Christ is our birth certificate.

> *It's adventurously expectant, greeting God with a child-like, "What's next, Papa?" God's Spirit touches our spirits and confirms who we really are. We know who he is, and we know who we are: Father and children. And we know we are going to get what's coming to us—an unbelievable inheritance!*
>
> ROMANS 8:16–17 THE MESSAGE

• *Children have simple trust.* When my father promised to bring me a surprise from his travels, I believed him. When parents tell children that on Christmas Eve an overstuffed, grandfatherly, white-bearded figure in red velvet named Santa Claus will descend into their fireplace—a place twice as small as its visitor—their eyes grow wide with wonder. Most believe their parents without hesitation. This same wonder-filled spirit in children allows them to believe that Moses truly crossed the Red Sea, that a big fish swallowed Jonah, and that Jesus died just for them. This childlike ability to take God at His Word is the same quality that opens the kingdom of heaven. How many of you trace your earliest spiritual beginnings to faith roots planted as a child?

"Of course there must be lots of Magic in the world," he said wisely one day, "but people don't know what it is like or how to make it."

FRANCES HODGSON BURNETT,
The Secret Garden

Young children know nothing of adult skepticism. Because of that, however, they are also easily swayed into believing the wrong things. What to put away? Gullible, childish beliefs that lead to disaster.

Dear children, keep yourselves from idols.
1 JOHN 5:21 NIV

Keep the ability to believe the impossible. Treasure simple trust and childlike faith. Jesus felt strongly about this.

But if you give them a hard time, bullying or taking
advantage of their simple trust, you'll soon wish
you hadn't.   MATTHEW 18:6 THE MESSAGE

For those who have squelched the innocence of children
with selfish, perverted behavior, and to those who have un-
wittingly tried to destroy the child in others instead of keeping it alive, Jesus has strong words. Perhaps He summed up
his fervent feelings about children in the following verses:

You'd be better off dropped in the middle of the lake with
a millstone around your neck. Doom to the world for giv-
ing these God-believing children a hard time! . . .Watch
that you don't treat a single one of these childlike believ-
ers arrogantly. You realize, don't you, that their personal
angels are constantly in touch with my Father in heaven?
                    MATTHEW 18:7, 10–11 THE MESSAGE

To both the abuser of children and the abused child, Jesus
offers restoration. For some, the child died long before they
reached adulthood. For them, childhood wonder is locked
inside fearful, poisoned minds that never learned to trust. Only
Jesus can breathe new life into that which was thought to be
dead. To all He freely declares:

I am, right now, Resurrection and Life. The one who
believes in me, even though he or she dies, will live.
                            JOHN 11:25 THE MESSAGE

When we finished our walk through the Bible, I sat motionless. I was so awed by Jesus' teaching, that I half expected Him to feed me on the spot by producing some miraculous loaves and fishes. His words convicted me to discard childish behaviors, but also to embrace childlike belief.

I sighed as I realized that at least a few of my furry creatures and childhood dolls would keep their permanent home in my decor and in my heart after all. Just to keep the child alive, you understand.

Master Designer Secret

"*The child is not dead but asleep.*"

MARK 5:39 NIV

Heart Check

What are you doing to keep the child alive in your heart?

Loving Touches

WHERE DOES THE WONDER BEGIN?

Where does the wonder begin for you?
In the pages of a book?
In a word, a song, in another's touch,
*   in the warmth of a loving look?*
Do you see with innocent eyes, unmarred
*   by wounded hearts and lenses?*
Is the wonder locked inside of you,
*   behind painted, barbed-wire fences?*
Can you dream once again as you hold the hand
*   of a child who's left in your care?*
Will you seek to unlock the mysteries of life?
Will you try? Yes, you can! Will you dare?
Yes, Virginia, there IS a magical cure
*   for the unbelieving heart.*
There is laughter and love and new dreams for the taking,
*   and God gives to each a part.*
For we are magicians here in this world,
*   to us are given the keys—*
And as long as we see with the eyes of a child,
*   the wonder will never cease.*

A Reflective Place

*When the heart is still
before the Creator,
the pen becomes a divine instrument,
both of blessing and of healing.*

Hang Familiar Pictures at Eye Level

Jesus headed through the hallway again, and we passed through a familiar gauntlet—my "Hall of Famely"—where almost all of our family pictures hang. But my Master Designer kept walking until He entered my bedroom. "It helps to keep pictures at eye level," He said with a twinkle in His eye.

Huh? I walked back into the hallway, glancing at those framed family members again. Yes, if someone were five feet ten inches, the pictures hung at eye level. I entered my bedroom, ready to protest, when I saw Jesus' eyes fixed on one corner of my bedroom. There, nestled cozily between a wicker chair and silk plant stood a simple pine desk. Scattered over the top were various pieces of mail to answer, my Bible, lamps, and a Victorian box filled with pens, pencils, bookmarks, extra batteries, and other sundry items. A gift from my mom, an antique inkwell, perched on a piece of faded lace. Next to it lay what I often refer to as the microphone of my soul—in this case, a calligraphy pen. Underneath my desk I kept an attractive, colorful binder, which I affectionately called the "pages of my heart."

Jesus stooped down, picked up one of my clothbound journals, and began thumbing through the pages. I still found no connection between His earlier comment and His present actions.

Those decorative journals had become good friends. Years ago, as an adolescent girl, I began recording personal impressions, starting first with the mundane activities of my life. As if engaged in some deep, dark ritual, I kept the secrets of my heart under lock and key away from prying, sibling eyes. Years later as a young mother, I tucked away my grins and groans and photographic memories of family life on notebook paper, stuffing them into disorderly file folders—tasty morsels for my homespun newspaper column at the time.

Keep your heart with all diligence, For out of it spring the issues of life.

PROVERBS 4:23 NKJV

My on-again, off-again journaling habits continued for several years. I graduated from scrap paper to cheap notebooks, many of which have long since fallen apart. And then one day I took a new direction.

On that particular occasion, my husband took me on a romantic weekend to a unique bed and breakfast. Stuffed full of *Victoria* magazines, dolls, bears, and "fru-fru" stuff—our cabin had my name all over it. But not a hundred yards away stood a masculine drawing card—one with Larry's name on it—a small lake and a boat for our use. It was a perfect couple's retreat.

We awoke early the next morning after arriving. Although I love fishing, I begged to stay behind until later in the day, while my husband cast a few lures from the aluminum boat nearby. I dressed and poured a leisurely cup of coffee. For a few precious moments I wanted to linger in the front porch rocker of this cottage hideaway, with pen and journal in hand. I needed a fresh beginning—to draw away for "longer hunks of time" as author Anne Ortlund once suggested.

With one daughter at the time living on her own and the other away at college, my nest was semi-empty. My yearning for simplicity and balance had only increased through the years, and I was determined to make a fresh start in still another way in my life, if even only a small one. With my Bible, a new calligraphy pen, and rose-covered journal in hand, I began to write. You must realize by now that I am a hopeless romantic—and a poet at heart. Here are sample notes from my journal that day:

New dreams often begin with new places. So here, in this "Heavenly Acres" hideaway, I shall begin a new thing— the process of birthing new dreams. I have read that journaling on temporary, ordinary notebooks that yellow and shred with age indicates how we view ourselves. So after years of scrawling hasty, barely legible notes that suggest feelings of inadequacy, I will start again.

As I read of Moses and the children of Israel crossing the Red Sea, I feel God has been leading me to a crossing as well—a parting of the waters. He has placed in my hand a rod, a tool with which to walk across. At times, I feel as if I am already on the other side, standing firmly on the shores of Canaan. Other times I have felt as though the waters raged on either side, ready to drown me. . . .

But today, the pillar of fire by night and the cloud by day will guide me, just as it did Moses and the Israelites, for I have crossed the waters. I have not arrived at my final destination, but I have waded through one step at a time to the other side. Now the decision is up to me. Where will I go? Where will these foolish thoughts take me? How big can we dream? Only you know, Lord. . . .

So here in this quiet place of retreat—here where my husband has surprised me on our twenty-eighth anniversary—here I will respect these gifts you have given me. Journal pages will no longer reflect a tattered book—a life, worn and brittle, rough, illegible, with ragged seams. From now on my journals will mirror dignity and worth and the priceless value of being loved as a precious child of God! I am Yours! I am a daughter of the King!

I am bound together, not by loose-leaf, yellowed pages, but I am constructed with care, woven and glued tightly together by a Master Artist and Creator. I will treat this gift of life—and these thoughts—as valuable and inspired, worthy of declaration, worthy of beauty, worthy of permanence—if only for Your heart and mine.

So, here is my life again, Lord—bruised, broken, but healed, a blank journal waiting to be filled with Your words, Your comfort, Your beauty, Your hope. What I write; what I dream; what I pursue will be like no other. For You have made me one of a kind, an awesome original.

Here in this 'Rose Cottage,' I begin a fresh page of my life. Here, with this man who has loved me, stood by me, and walked through deep waters with me for twenty-eight years of marriage. Let them be our dreams, Lord.

Let me not run rampant with my tangents, like a kite on the loose, but help each of us to pursue mutual dreams. Fit our lives together, Lord, into a pattern that pleases You. Form our ministry into a God-thing—something only You can do.

Begin a new thing today, Lord. Form new, permanent dreams. You came to make our joy full!

There is a delicious gladness that comes from God. A holy joy. A sacred delight. It is within your reach.

MAX LUCADO,
The Applause of Heaven

And that can only happen in You. I agree with Helen Keller, Lord, "No pessimist ever discovered the secrets of the stars, or sailed to an uncharted land, or opened a new heaven to the human spirit." Life is not to be lived in pessimistic pursuits, but with gratefulness and abundant joy!

—♁

Familiar moments. Familiar pictures. "Oh," I said thoughtfully. I was beginning to understand. How would it help me to write my thoughts if I never looked at them again? Occasionally, I had flipped through my journals when searching for a specific illustration—and in the past I had even spent a few Sunday afternoons reviewing the previous week's entries. But not consistently. And besides, some years were too painful to reopen. Didn't the apostle Paul himself say, "Forgetting what is behind. . .I press on. . . ." (Have you noticed how we can always use Scripture to justify our case?)

Who has time anymore? I reasoned. *I'm doing pretty good just journaling. Most people don't even do that. And for what reason would I conduct this ongoing ritual of review?* I was about to find out.

Together, my Master Designer and I began to sift through the pages of my heart. As we thumbed through past years, I realized my journals contained more than pen and ink. Like a maze, they provide the clues—and weave a path through my own spiritual journey.

One year I felt the need for personal counseling. I was excited to hear my counselor's homework assignment for that week: "Write out the feelings of your heart in your journal— what you are going through."

I could do that! Writing—and especially journaling— had always been a catharsis for me. In times of confusion or wanderlust I had discovered in my journals the jewels Russell H. Conwell once referred to: "Your diamonds are not in far distant mountains or in yonder seas; they are in your own backyard, if you but dig for them."

As Jesus and I began "digging" through those recorded memories and impressions, I found shining nuggets of inspiration again and a trail of learned wisdom that once more led me back to the Author of my life. I had almost forgotten those lessons. There, I saw the tracks of God's faithfulness in virtual black and white. Fears vanished, and worries faded when I reviewed my notes of how God often answered—and blessed—again and again. Familiar pictures. Familiar stories. Opened and "hung" where the eye can see and review and where the heart can give thanks once again.

Do I keep all the pages of my heart? No, some, written during angry outbursts of my spirit, cease to serve a good purpose. Once I can see the scathing emotions lurking beneath the surface, confession brings healing. Forgiveness flows, and I bury those pages in the city dump.

But now you must rid yourselves of all such things as these: anger, rage, malice. . . .

COLOSSIANS 3:8 NIV

⸺ဢ

Do the pages of your heart flutter and beg for affirmation? Have you taken time to record the jewels God gives you? Some of the best advice I ever read as a young mother came from Anne Ortlund's book, *Disciplines of a Beautiful Woman.* She encourages women to carve out time to write goals and dreams and to let God speak to them by taking an entire day or half a day to get away.

I packed up my Bible and notebook and tried that one year when my children attended elementary school. For four delicious hours at a nearby park I wrote, prayed, listened, and ate from God's hand. So gratifying was that experience, it became a frequent practice through the years. Now that my children are grown and married, the journals fill up quickly, and strangely enough, the need to record my heart's deepest cravings is greater than ever. Journaling forces me to stop and focus again on what God has called me to do.

After returning home from that romantic hideaway years ago, I made another decision. As I began writing in my new, attractive journals, I slowed down my pen—deliberately. Not to preserve legible words for my future grandchildren (though with my handwriting, God knows they will need help), but to take seriously the thoughts God gives me—and perhaps take another baby step toward simplifying my life.

Have you misplaced the pages of your heart? Are there some pieces missing? Are there forgotten lessons and bestowed blessings buried beneath the surface of your heart? Buy your favorite style journal; head out to the backyard, a nearby lake, or even your bedroom. Grab your Bible, a good pen, and "go digging." You might just discover a gold mine inside.

Master Designer Secret

My heart is overflowing. . .
My tongue is the pen
of a ready writer.

PSALM 45:1 NKJV

Heart Check

*What blessings do you need to record
today in the "pages of your heart"?*

THOUGHTS ON JOURNALING

If you have never tried to journal, here are some ideas. At different times, you will use various methods of journaling. As you begin to record your thoughts, try some of the following suggestions if you need help:

- Buy an affordable but attractive bound journal, one that reflects your tastes.
- Look at your calendar. Ask a friend to baby-sit or offer to swap off times with a friend to keep each other's children. Then pencil in a specific date and carve out a few hours to spend alone with two friends: your journal and the Lord.
- Open your Bible to a favorite chapter, or let God direct you to a passage of Scripture. Read it over several times, asking God to speak to your heart. As you begin to journal, take a few moments just to listen. Assuming you are outside (but not necessarily), what do you hear? Write it down. What is God saying to you in these verses of Scripture? Write it down. (Later you may want

to use a separate journal for recording your thoughts from Scripture.)

- What are you feeling right now? About your life? About your relationships? About the Lord? Write it down. What do you see? Describe what you see by how it feels to the touch. What word pictures can you give to what you feel, hear, or see? Involve the senses. Write down your impressions.
- Think about the last week or the last few months. How has God been working in your life? What lessons has He taught you? What blessings has He given you? Record these in your journal.
- What obstacles are you facing right now? What would you like for God to do for you, your family, for others on your heart?
- What are your goals for the future? What are your dreams?
- Determine to set a daily time if possible; if not, take whatever time you can to write in your journal, using several of the above suggestions. At least once a week, read through what you have written in the last week or two.
- Once in awhile, thumb back further through the years. Remember, the purpose is not to stir up painful memories, however, but to review a track record of God's faithfulness. Make sure you meditate on "whatever things are pure, lovely, excellent or praiseworthy" (Philippians 4:8 NIV, author's paraphase).

A Balanced Place

*We hear God best
when our hearts are at rest.*

Leave Plenty of Open Spaces

Our tour was drawing to a close. Jesus had chosen a renovation program—not at all like mine. I had visualized furniture changes, new paint jobs, new add-ons. But as I thought back over my life, I realized He had walked through my home many times, making drastic changes. I just didn't recognize His work at the time.

Jesus paused, took one more look around, then opened the back door of my home. I followed Him as we stepped onto the hard concrete patio. I had grown to love this small backyard retreat—a place where I could draw near to my Master and still the distracting voices inside my heart. I wondered silently how Jesus would change this beloved place of mine.

I looked around, noting the "furnishings" of my retreat. My porch swing is retired—for now. A patio stretches into our small backyard, but the roof is not strong enough to support a swing. So after ten years of nonuse, that swing waits in the tool shed for a new frame. My husband says a gazebo would dwarf such a small space, but someday I still hope to build one if we

Through God's creation, we can hear the gentle whispers of His own heart, inviting us to rest quietly in His love.

ever move to another house. At every camp, retreat center, or bed and breakfast where we've stayed, I always find my way out to a gazebo hideaway. That miniature escape is my thinking, reflecting, meditating garden. There, I grow all kinds of organic dreams and schemes. Some of these will wither and die; others will push their way to the surface and await harvest.

Soon after moving here, I had convinced Larry to hang a hammock between two big trees in our tiny backyard—swaying across a blanket of green ivy. There, in beautiful weather or cool, early mornings, I loved to meet the Creator and relax. I'd close my eyes, and the soft, rocking motions reminded me of my Father's gentle arms.

Mentally, I rehearsed my favorite ritual: For a few moments, maybe even an hour if I'm so inclined in the early mornings, I let time stand still and marvel at the beauty of God's creation. A cardinal and blue jay race to the feeder to see who will win the prize nugget. A noisy squirrel follows, hanging upside down like a monkey to scarf up the scattered sunflower seeds. He swishes his tail with uncanny rhythm, as if to some unsung melody, heard only by his ears. The sweetness of jasmine gently blows by overhead.

There, for awhile in my hammock, I add "margin," a principle advocated by Dr. Richard Swenson. He believes "margin" is the necessary ingredient in creating emotional, physical, financial, and time reserves that every person needs.

Marginless, Swenson says, *is being thirty minutes late to work or the doctor's office because you were twenty minutes late getting out of the hairdresser's because you were ten minutes late dropping the children off at school because the car ran out of gas two blocks from the gas station—and you forgot your purse.*

Margin, on the other hand, is having breath left at the top of the staircase, money left at the end of the month, and sanity left at the end of adolescence.

Marginless is the baby crying and the phone ringing at the same time; margin is Grandma taking the baby for the afternoon.

Marginless is not having time to finish the book you're reading on stress; margin is having the time to read it twice.[IX]

My thoughts took a detour for a moment, as guilt tried to sway my reasoning. *There are other ways I still need to add margin. Maybe Jesus wants to talk to me about that.*

I would never win the "early bird" award, but I am usually punctual. Larry says I see arriving early somewhere as a waste of creative time. He may be right. But I can still change. Like a page without margins, I stuff my life full of good things—just not always the best. Like clockwork, each year rolls out new challenges and opportunities. I want to try them all, and the choices are maddening.

Which ones deserve my time and attention? Which ones are not only the longings of my heart, but more importantly, the desires of God's own heart?

What about the gifts God gives us? I cannot develop every ability, every seed into a full-grown flower, when my garden is already full. Then will God remove what I do not use?

Many suggest that quiet times are merely fifteen-minute sessions to begin the day. However, on some days, I am so thirsty, I drink for over an hour. Often, I spend much of that time in my own wistful wanderings and longings to know the heart of God—and make sure He understands mine. Yet the need to pray earnestly for others calls me as well.

Letters wait for acknowledgment; friends need encouragement; a house cries for overhaul. Clothes beg for ironing; meals call for planning and preparation; kindness wants to be lavished on the objects of our affection. Projects deserve their completion; articles scream, "Write me!" Hungry souls need nourishment; students thirst for knowledge. Disciples want to grow; books groan for birthing. Children need to be blossomed; parents and siblings wait for our love; closets demand organization; talents beg for development. The guilt trip continues unmercifully down a stream of accusing, rocky obstacles, as I realize the mountain of responsibility awaiting me daily.

Am I not using those talents, after all? I am teaching an adult Bible study class. I am singing in choir, making melody in my heart. I am encouraging and discipling. I am reading constantly to improve my knowledge. I am in God's Word daily. I am seeking to meet some of the needs of my husband and family, knowing God must meet the rest.

I am "creating" something often—whether it is a grapevine wreath for the wall, a word picture on paper, a new idea, or a fragrant blossom in someone's life. I try to keep abreast of world events and pray for the injustice I see. My heart yearns with compassion as I wish I could feed and clothe all the hungry and the poor of our world. But I cannot do it all or be it all. I could never give enough to a holy God worthy of so much. But perhaps God didn't ask me to do it all.

For a moment I felt as if I had slipped into Joan's life and lost Baby Grace, too. Suddenly I felt a divine finger silencing my lips and quelling my imaginary debate, a quieter voice restoring my longings, pushing me into His presence.

There is no mode of life in the world more pleasing and more full of delight than continual conversation with God.

BROTHER LAWRENCE

"Leave plenty of open spaces," Jesus replied to my questioned thoughts. "Remember, balance is good for the soul, too." Perhaps those open spaces I leave—the margins God helps me to create—call me back and return my thoughts to a God who loves me as I am. It is a safe place—a place of balance.

Like a page out of my notebook, margins give the senses a place to pause. The eyes can rest a moment before racing to the next finish line of new sentences. Margin creates a pause in my spirit, a check that helps me refocus on God's true character, not on my performance.

⌒

The conclusions are simple. My real gazebo is here—no, not in a hammock—but here at the feet of Jesus—here in my home in the pages of everyday love and life. For it is here that I find the real joy in the lessons of simplicity and margin—this stripping away of layers to the bare essentials of ministry and life.

Here I find the mysterious principle of addition plus subtraction equals multiplication. For I may have subtracted one hour of my day. But I am amazed to see in reality I have added much more than twenty-four. Like Jesus' miracle as He multiplied the loaves and fishes to feed thousands of followers, I have basketfuls of good things to give away—and they are not even leftovers. They are the choicest morsels I could serve a waiting world and family.

It is a principle Jesus has been trying to instill into every room of my heart.

Master Designer Secret

He makes me lie down
in green pastures. . .
he restores my soul.

PSALM 23:2–3 NIV

Heart Check

Is there an area out of balance right now?
How can you add margin to your life?

Loving Touches

MARGIN

The pause that refreshes,
A pull to look up,
A prodding to linger for a second cup—
A prescription for pain,
formed by layers of stress,
Permission to walk in green meadows and rest—
The pathway of blessing,
A plan to create,
A passion for love, a buffer for hate—
Prizing relationships,
Providing reserves,
Giving priorities the time they deserve—
Practicing patience,
Partitioning time,
Preserving fresh memories while still in my prime—
Pruning the excess baggage of life,
Pursuing the joy of just being alive,
The planting of dreams in available soil—
Parking my thoughts for complete overhaul.

YOU KNOW YOUR LIFE IS OUT OF BALANCE WHEN. . .

- On Sunday mornings your husband asks if he has a shirt clean, and you remember you forgot to pick them up at the cleaner's a week ago.

- You offer to read your child a bedtime story—on her thirteenth birthday.
- You pray, "Lord, direct my steps today," and then drive ten miles out of the way to avoid seeing a neighbor you dislike.
- Your friends can't remember your name or address.
- A friend calls you for a favor in January—and you're booked until December.
- The theme song of your marriage changes from "I Honestly Love You" to "You Don't Bring Me Flowers Anymore."
- Your children can't remember the last time that they heard "I love you."
- When PMS lasts four weeks out of the month.
- Your communication with your family consists only of imperatives such as "Don't! Watch It! Hurry up!"
- You know more about the president's personal life than your own family's.
- You need a vacation—after your vacation.
- Your children ask you to find the book of Joshua for them, and you reply, "If you can't keep up with your friend's books, then quit borrowing them."

A Holy Place

*Home
is where God is.*

Create Private Sanctuaries

Before we left the backyard, Jesus spoke again. "Come, let's take a walk," He said. "I'd like to see your garden."

Years ago, one of the things I anticipated most about owning my first home was growing a garden. And not just an ordinary, run-of-the-mill garden. I dreamed of a floral sanctuary, right out of the pages of *Better Homes and Gardens*. I'd plant old English roses, prize tulips, fancy irises, and a yellow carpet of sun-loving daffodils. After all, "Time began in the Garden," as Emilie Barnes so aptly said.

I would have loved tending that first beautiful Garden in Eden, where unhindered beauty and fellowship first grew in a sinless world. How awesome to walk and talk with the Creator of the Universe in the cool of a perfect garden—a place with no thorns and no weeds—planted with God's own hands. How sweet to share your heart in the garden with God.

Throughout Jesus' ministry, He talked about gardens. In Matthew 13 and 20, this place could be a home for God's created beauty, a haven of worship for birds, and a symbol of faith for the believer (mustard seed). Christ referred to Himself as the Vine and to His Father as the Gardener (John 15:1). And Scripture very beautifully called Jesus the "Lily of the Valley" and the "Rose of Sharon" (Song of Solomon 2:1).

Jesus used common parables about the garden. He chose farming terms and compared the godly man as one "planted by the rivers of water" (Psalm 1:3 NKJV). In the Garden of Gethsemane Jesus spent many precious hours, pouring out His heart and lifeblood with His heavenly Father. My husband and I visited Israel many years ago. What an awesome experience to walk in that garden and then to peer into the empty tomb where Jesus' body was buried and resurrected. The garden—what a holy, symbolic place.

But why would Jesus want to see my garden? I thought again of my lofty dreams and garden ambitions. Unfortunately, my early years of child rearing and ministry allowed me only scattered moments to indulge my secret passion. Wherever we lived, my best efforts brought only a few roses, some periwinkles that popped up every year, an assortment of green hanging plants, and a few bedraggled petunias. Inevitably every February—when the first splashes of color appeared in my neighbors' yards—I remembered too late that I forgot to plant mine in fall.

The backyard of my current house is one of the reasons I loved and chose our home. It was small, but I could visualize a garden for every season. I drew up schemes and plans for months, scouring magazines and bending the ears of our local nursery owners. Soon my garden ideas filled an entire box.

"It's just an ordinary garden. Nothing special. And it's not finished yet," I hastily apologized to Jesus. "But let me go get my plans. I know You'll like them."

"That isn't necessary. Let's just walk—and talk."

I felt as if I had just walked into the studio of C. Austin Miles, the songwriter who penned the familiar words and music of the great hymn, "In the Garden."

This morning the dew was still fresh, like the song said. And Jesus and I had walked here together often. But as we approached my roses, I felt another stale apology rising to the surface. My garden dreams had somehow exceeded my strength. I so wanted a green thumb like my father's or to grow prize

> *We have a faithful Gardener who waits at the garden gate each morning, tools ready, sleeves rolled up.*
>
> GIGI TCHIVIDJIAN GRAHAM,
> *Passing It On*

roses like my brother. Each season I had accomplished a little but soon discovered a change was necessary.

Reluctantly I reduced my Victorian garden to small plots scattered over the backyard. My husband agreed to help. Together, we spent hours planting a rose garden on the east side of the house. Towering oaks shaded the rose bed a bit too much. Still, for a few years, I managed to pick a few dozen rosebuds to grace my table.

"There's nothing extraordinary about my garden," I repeated, more emphatically. As we approached my thorny rose bushes, I stuttered my apology to Jesus. "I. . .uh. . .it. . .uh. . .the roses haven't done so well." The spindly stalks looked pitiful and untended. "I've been a little busy. They're not very beautiful right now, are they?"

"They need more sun," said Jesus. "And pruning." I was afraid He'd curse them on the spot for being unproductive, just like He had done with that fruitless fig tree in the Bible. Instead, from His garment He pulled out a large pair of pruning shears and began lopping off the scraggly limbs of my rose bushes. I watched, horrified, as He cut my beloved roses down to ugly stumps.

"But. . . ," I started to protest. He was already moving on.

I glanced at the rest of my garden before following Jesus along the gravel path. In another area, we had prepared a small bed soon after moving into our home. There I had gingerly plopped six or seven dozen bulbs into the ground. Then I sat back and waited. And waited. And waited. Finally, a tiny spot of yellow announced spring's arrival. "Larry!" I yelled as I looked out my bedroom window one sunny morning. "Come quick! A daffodil! Our first daffodil!"

Each day my excitement grew. Within a couple of weeks, most of the bulbs had filled their assigned home with vivid color. And then they were gone, leaving only limp, yellowing stalks in their place.

Jesus now stood in front of that pale flowerbed. Mondo grass had spread its shoots like an infiltrating enemy, and weeds had almost covered the faded bulbs' stalks. I hung my head and offered a lame excuse. "The flowers didn't last long."

"There's a season for everything," Jesus replied. And with one sweep of His hand, He yanked the weeds and excess grass out of their temporary home. And walked on.

I was about to follow Him to the next spot when something caught my attention. A butterfly hung suspended in midair. Shimmering in the sun, like a ladder of dew-dropped pearls, hung an almost invisible net. I watched the butterfly struggle a few seconds before surrendering to its enemy's trap. The spider was winning, and I didn't like it. I thought of the struggle this winged insect had gone through just to escape its cocoon. Yes, I know about the food chain. But I couldn't bear to see such a beautiful creature die so soon. Why couldn't the spider pick on something its own size—like a nasty old fly?

Some butterflies spring from their cocoons in just a few days; others struggle for years before finding their wings.

Country Living

Jesus turned and walked back to where I stood. "Wings were made for flying," He said. And gently, carefully, He plucked the fluttering insect from inevitable destruction. I watched Him as He lifted the creature toward the sky—and onto a higher destination.

"Come," He said. "There's more to see." He brought me full circle again to the garden area near the hammock.

My husband had painstakingly built me a brick tree ring around the large tree that anchored the hammock. There I planted my perennial plants: variegated hostas, fragile ferns, and an assortment of guaranteed-to-grow-even-if-you-leave-them-alone type plants.

I had watched as tiny green leaves began to sprout, and for awhile the plants flourished. But some city personnel trouped through my backyard one day and cut down several huge limbs of my beloved shade tree. The branches had grown too close to the electrical lines. That exposed my shade-loving ferns to the sun's full rays, and even the hardy, impossible-to-kill hostas struggled to survive.

We stood before the tree ring, and this time I had no excuses. Jesus just smiled, took my hand, and said tenderly, "They will return—in the spring. Everything is beautiful in its time." And He turned back to the patio, pulled up a chair, and sat down.

What did all that mean? I thought.

I looked at Jesus. His very posture said to me, "There's something more you need to see."

So I retraced our steps in the garden. *Was there a missing piece to this puzzle?* I walked back to the rose bushes that stood now as naked, unproductive stumps. I'd spent hours savoring my precious roses. Each petal had become a symbol to me of beauty—of what I wanted my garden and my life to represent. I had sprayed for pesky insects, watered during drought, and fed them with ample doses of fertilizer to increase their blooms. From the first day they were planted, I had even knelt and dedicated these beautiful plants to the Lord. Yet they yielded only puny blooms. What went wrong?

Jesus' words kept echoing through my mind: *They need more sun—and pruning.* I thought of Job, a righteous man in the Bible, who endured God's testing of faith—a painful pruning process. The loss of everything dear and precious to him reduced this saint to a stump of a man. Yet he blessed God, and eventually God restored to him even more than he once had.

And I remembered Jesus' two disciples who also experienced Jesus' pruning. James and John, prodded by an overeager mom, vied for a place in the kingdom on either side of Jesus. But a few words from the Master sliced through their ambitious pride and trimmed them down to size. They needed more of the Son.

What about me? How could I expect my puny efforts to produce a beautiful bouquet for the Lord without adequate doses of the Son? Why should I object if Jesus wanted to prune back every branch of my life to produce more blooms? I moved on to the next spot, but first made two commitments: (1) I would move my roses to a sunny bed, and (2) I would be more faithful to prune them each season.

"Every branch that does bear fruit he prunes so that it will be even more fruitful."

JOHN 15:2 NIV

Next stop, the bulb garden. What had Jesus said? *There's a season for everything.*

A poem I had written in my journal a few years ago expressed what I felt as I looked at this lifeless mess before me:

What season is it now, Lord?
Winter, fall, spring?
A time to hibernate and rest?
A time for me to sing?
How do I fit into Your scheme?
When will this season pass?
How long before You answer?
How long will this time last?
The seeds have long been planted;
My roots are growing deep.
But the leaves are turning yellow;
How long before I reap?

The weeds have choked their years from me;
I need the springtime rain.
I long to see new flowers bloom
Where once grew only pain.
I cannot make a garden
By struggling on my own;
But I can lift my branches high,
And let You bring the growth.

One particular season of my life involved endless changes. Yet spring still followed, yielding new dreams. As always, God was faithful to do His part.

I walked by the silver spider web still hanging from the eaves of the house. My heart began to flutter with excitement—just like that butterfly Jesus had freed. I was beginning to understand the thread of Jesus' words—the reason for our tour of the garden. Hadn't He repeatedly released my life from dreaded strongholds?

Even then, I was struggling with a new opportunity to serve Him, and fear was holding me prisoner. Jesus was calling for my obedience—and an abandoned spirit that joined with Isaiah crying, "Here am I. Send me." But I had health concerns. My confidence was shaky. And how could I add one more thing to an already full schedule? But His gentle message to my heart was unmistakable: "Winter is past. Springtime is here. Rebecca, it's time to fly."

I returned to the last stop on our tour and looked at the dying plants surrounding my tree ring. But this time I audibly affirmed Jesus' words. "Everything *will* become beautiful in *His* time."

In less than thirty minutes, Jesus had given me a pictorial overview of my life. I was a woman given to lofty dreams. At times it seemed as if life chopped those dreams to barely recognizable stubs. But as I looked back, I could now see and understand what a difference the Son had made in my life—even when the circumstances didn't turn out in my favor.

My father once said to me, "Some dreams have to die." And some did. Others hung on, suspended in my life for years before God brought them to pass. Years ago I first dreamed about writing a book. I found a promise in Habbakuk 2:2–3 (TLB) and asked God if I could make it my own:

> *Even when we cannot see the why and the wherefore of God's dealings, we know that there is love in and behind them, and so we can rejoice always, even when, humanly speaking, things are going wrong.*
>
> J. I. PACKER,
> *Knowing God*

Write my answer on a billboard, large and clear, so that anyone can read it at a glance and rush to tell the others. But these things I plan won't happen right away. Slowly, steadily, surely, the time approaches when the vision will be fulfilled. If it seems slow, do not despair, for these things will surely come to pass. Just be patient! They will not be overdue a single day!

I reviewed those verses often, thanking God for the time when He would fulfill my "vision." I had read more than once about how extraordinary dreams were born from ordinary visions.

> *"Writing is like a 'lust,' or like 'scratching when you itch.' Writing comes as a result of a very strong impulse, and when it does come, I for one must get it out."*
>
> C. S. LEWIS,
> *Getting Into Print,*
> by SHERWOOD E. WIRT

For years, my writing took a different direction than I expected—greeting cards, articles, stories, calendars —whatever fed my writing hunger and brought income. But I kept planting "bulbs" of book ideas into my file folder and into the mailbox. Hopes would spring up and then die again as I harvested one rejection after another. At times the weeds of discontent tried to choke out my effectiveness. Eventually, my book ideas began to take root in editors' hearts. I realize now, many seasons—especially winters—had to pass before my time of harvest would appear. But there was indeed a reason—and a season—for everything that God had allowed in my life.

When I was a young mom, eager to launch my big dreams but frustrated by the inability to do so, Mom offered some wise advice: "Rebecca, take care of the most important things right now. Later, you will have more time to write—and more to write about." She was right. The interesting thing is that by the time I reached that stage, those dreams seemed less important.

Jesus wanted to make sure I understood. All through our tour, He kept repeating: "Only one thing is needed." He was reemphasizing to me that that one thing was the relationship with Jesus Himself.

There was something more I needed to do. I walked over to where Jesus was sitting. I had no expensive fragrance to pour on Jesus' feet. My bottle of White Shoulders perfume had only a few drops left. And my beautician had reduced my long locks to a curly bob. But I knelt at Jesus' feet, with hands outstretched like an adoring child waiting to be held by her father, and with tears of gratefulness and praise, I worshipped the Rose of Sharon, the King of Kings, the Name above All Names. I felt His hand upon my head and His touch upon my heart.

Surely, praise—as well as time—must have begun in a garden, too. From this point on, my heart—and my garden—would be a holy place, a sanctuary where I could join all of nature often in affirming, "Let everything that has breath praise the Lord" (Psalm 150:6 NIV).

⁓

In the weeks and months that followed that experience, my garden grew. Not necessarily with colorful flowers, though I did purchase some hearty pots of color to brighten up the landscape. We moved some of the roses and even bought more to plant in a new rose garden by the fence—a place where the morning sun would hit more frequently, though still not completely. Ultimately, I may have to postpone the dream of a flourishing Victorian rose garden—to another time, another home, another place—where full sun can indeed nourish its roots. Or God may require I give up the notion entirely. And I can accept that. After all, God didn't promise me a rose garden.

But in the meantime I've been adding something more to my garden. As much as I like colorful, growing plants, I discovered I also enjoyed garden art. Each piece I purchased created not a shrine, but a sanctuary—a place to remind me of our encounters in the garden—and of a Holy God. A birdbath symbolizes Living Water that both refreshes the fowl of the air and nourishes parched human hearts. A gazing ball reflects at a glance the beauty of God's creation and reminds me that I, too, am a reflection of His glory. And in both an aging wicker chair and an iron, antique settle rest colorful pots of seasonal flowers, beckoning me to sit awhile and enjoy His presence.

To further celebrate the lessons I had learned—and a commitment I had made that day in the garden with Jesus— I did something both unusual and spontaneous. When our pastor spoke one Sunday about Moses' call from God and his experience with the burning bush, I couldn't sit still. The words of that Scripture burned my heart just like the fire from the angel's tongs on Isaiah's lips (Isaiah 6:1–7). " 'Do not come any closer,' God said [to Moses]. 'Take off your sandals, for the place where you are standing is holy ground' " (Exodus 3:5 NIV).

When the invitation time came, I removed my sandals, grabbed my minister husband's hand, and together we knelt at the altar. "Will you pray for me?" I pleaded. And with one hand in his and the other raised toward heaven, I celebrated— and sealed—my answer to God concerning the issue I struggled with that day in the garden. Even though I had been teaching Bible studies for over twenty-five years and speaking at various events for some time, I had decided to refresh my skills and again go back to the basics. I attended a popular speaker's training seminar that very weekend—"just to see if God really does want me to do more of this."

Blessed are the people who know the passwords of praise, who shout on parade in the bright presence of God.

PSALM 89:15
THE MESSAGE

God had given me almost a dozen confirmations that weekend, culminating with the morning sermon. Whatever God chose to do with my commitment was immaterial. I had done my part. And at that moment, I knew I was standing on holy ground.

―∽

I'm well aware that reading a book like this is like stepping into someone's personal journal. And throughout our tour, I've been asking myself, "Why would you care? More importantly, is there anything here that applies to you?"

Only you can answer that. You may dislike gardening. But I bet you have some dreams. As women, we may not walk in

It's never too late to become what you might have been.

GEORGE ELIOT

the same season of life together. But some of you may feel like spring will never come. Some of you are fluttering your wings and feel trapped in a hopeless web of circumstances. You're about to give up the struggle. Others of you are wrestling with decisions too heady to handle. Praise eludes your lips like the sun on a cloudy day. Right now your heart—and maybe your home—feel like anything *but* a holy place. And you just don't feel like worshipping. Haven't we all been there—often?

In the midst of it all, would you just for a moment, as an act of simple obedience and faith, take a walk in the garden with Jesus, if only in your mind? Worship does not begin with the first note of a church organ—or even with the first step into His garden. Worship is the heart's plea for God, the cry of a spirit parched from the desert's heat. It may put a hallelujah on our lips with joyous jubilation. Or it may cause us to fall on our face with sincere consecration. Worship is believing God for who He is and trusting Him for what He will be.

Worship releases the spirit in bondage and frees the soul long in distress. Praise cries, "Abba," unashamedly to the Father. It reaches out with open arms to embrace the God of Love. With the silence of a quiet heart, worship hushes in His presence, yet leaps to sing His name. Best Friend, Faithful One, Redeemer and Lord—worship cannot speak adequately of the attributes of God, for His goodness exceeds all our dreams, our hopes, our expectations.

Worship is blessing, believing, and declaring God's

faithfulness, mercy, and grace—regardless of where or who we are. It is loving the One who first loved us.

As you walk through your imaginary, secret garden with Jesus, remember that worship is often a *sacrifice* of praise. That means offering ourselves to God whether we feel like it or not. Why do that? Because God inhabits the praises of His people (Psalm 22:3). His children speak their praise to the Father; and He ushers in His holiness, into our lives, and into that situation. Our hearts become living sanctuaries for His presence, and our whole perspective changes.

When that happens, we can do no less than remove our shoes. For we will indeed be standing on holy ground.

―࿔

Master Designer Secret

Come, let us bow down in worship,
let us kneel before the Lord our Maker.

PSALM 95:6 NIV

Heart Check

Is your heart a sanctuary for the Lord?

Loving Touches

IN THE GARDEN WITH GOD

When we walk in the garden with God each day,
There's a sweet perfume, like a rose-filled spray.
In those velvet soft moments, Nature hushes as He
Whispers gently, "I love you. Come and talk with me."
There by His side we grow closer together,
As we walk in the garden through all kinds of weather.
And the thorns of this life lose their hold as He
Whispers gently, "I love you. Come and walk with me."

A Heavenly Minded Place

No one's well has ever
run dry from giving
a cup of kindness to another.

Expand the Walls

It all started out as an attempt to measure up to that "Proverbs 31" woman image. Determined not to let ordinary work keep me from simple delights, I started rolling out pie dough when my girls were just toddlers. I discovered a melt-in-your-mouth flaky oil and milk crust that cut the time of pie making in half. Pies were a frequent love gift to my family—a symbol of simplicity on busy days.

Each time a new neighbor moved into my neighborhood or a friend emerged from the hospital, my "no fail" apple pie traveled to new homes. I had few dishes branded as my "specialty," but my fruit pies continued to bring rave reviews. It was a small way I could share Jesus' love with others. Perhaps this activity also symbolized to me the joy of being a homemaker—and the freedom to choose staying at home.

Years passed, and I was faced with a dilemma. Two girls in college simultaneously played havoc with our finances. My husband and I had been watching our savings dwindle for months, so we prayed about outside employment. My writing income had not yet reached my financial goals, so I signed up with a temporary agency. "Lord, if I have to work, put me where I can be salt and light," I prayed. "Let me make a difference somewhere!" ("And please, let it be a low-stress job!" I added.)

Sometimes God waits to answer until we stop and listen.

Except for three or four months of temporary part-time employment, I had not worked outside my home for seventeen years. I struggled for months, asking the Lord, "Are You sure this is what we need to do?" The creative part of me secretly longed to squelch a submissive spirit and cry out, "I have dreams, too!" *How could my writing make a difference in people's lives if I opted for outside work and had no energy left for my craft?*

My temporary secretarial job would last two months—a *high-stress, fast-paced,* forty-hour-a-week job. Could I handle it? I asked the young woman I would be working for why she chose me when others exceeded my qualifications.

"Because of your hands-on experience," she said.

I breathed a short prayer. *Thank You, Lord, for helping me keep up my computer skills.*

"And because you weren't fake," she continued.

That increased my confidence, but I still wondered why the Lord put me there. I longed to be home again, writing with my own free time.

I trained for three weeks until Lana, the girl I replaced, left to deliver her baby. For six weeks I prayed constantly that God would make me a witness.

I brought a rose from my garden each day. "It's to help me

222

remember to stop and smell the roses," I chirped meekly, when others commented. I felt like a remnant from Grandma's attic but kept smiling. When someone needed a lift, I "planted" my rose vase on their desk for the day. I was getting discouraged, however, at my seeming lack of influence, when God seemed to whisper, "What about your pies?" So on coworkers' birthdays, I made my "no fail" apple pie for the strangers I had just met. They asked me why. "Just because I wanted to and because you're special," I'd reply.

My cheerfulness swayed no one. "You know why she's sitting over there smiling, don't you?" someone accused. "It's because she's only temporary. She knows she'll leave this job soon."

Surrounding my cubicle I had placed personal reminders to help me keep my perspective: "I am only a temporary here; someday I'm going back home. Likewise, I am only temporary on this earth; someday I'm going home to my Heavenly Father." I included a favorite promise of mine, "I can do all things through Christ who strengthens me" (Philippians 4:13 NKJV). I invited coworkers to our church luncheons. Only one woman came. I listened to others' problems and complaints. And I continued to call Lana after she delivered her baby.

Due to some physical problems and pending tests, my doctor chose this time to take me off all medication. With a sprained back, no hormone replacement, and little sleep, I had difficulty coping. At work, my boss introduced me to a new computer program with a hasty five-minute lesson, then abandoned me. I grabbed every coworker who passed my desk and asked for help.

I followed precise instructions from Lana on copying

transparencies, but burned up the company's copy machine in the middle of a massive printing project. Each time I heard groans from the copy room, I slunk down in my secretarial chair, hoping no one would see my telltale guilt. "This is *not* the kind of difference I wanted to make, Lord," I cried.

When my boss asked me to hold all calls and visitors one day, I listened while an abusive customer chewed me out in front of other coworkers and patrons when he couldn't talk to my boss. I smiled, held myself together, then exited to the break room and fell apart.

I tried to get to know my fellow employees, asking God to share His love through me. "I'm not asking for notches on my belt, God," I prayed. "I only want to share Jesus in a natural way." I continued to bake pies and place them on unsuspecting coworkers' desks.

The secretarial job finally ended. I vowed to end outside work. . .at least for awhile. "I feel like a flop," I moaned to my husband. "I wanted to be a good example, but I barely kept my own faith together!" As usual, I set my expectations too high.

I determined to cultivate my new friendship with Lana, so I called her about a week after she returned to work. Her sister, Dana, had consulted a doctor for a routine sinus problem. The doctor sent her to a neurologist immediately. The prognosis? A brain tumor. Terminal. Immediate surgery.

My husband and I began to pray for Dana and decided to visit her with the family's permission. They had no minister. And they attended no church.

We walked in one evening to Dana's crowded hospital room. The tiny room and sterile hospital bed stood in stark contrast to the warm "birthing" suite where we had visited her sister, Lana, only weeks earlier.

"I came to tell you how you can invite Jesus into your life, Dana," said my husband. "To tell you how you can have peace. Do you mind if I share that with you?"

"Nooo," she drawled. She smiled a mischievous grin, wrinkling the white patch on her right eye. A massive bandage covered most of her head following the brain surgery. "And if anyone objects. . .they. . .can just. . .leave the room," she added.

No one left, so my husband shared simply how Dana could have peace with God. He knew death could claim her within days, so he felt free to emphasize the urgency of her decision.

"Would you like to have this peace, Dana?" he concluded. "Would you like to invite Jesus into your heart?"

She nodded tearfully.

He clarified the invitation repeatedly, making sure she understood. "If any of you want to pray with Dana, you can also find peace with God tonight," my husband added to the others in the room.

Dana repeated the words of the prayer slowly and deliberately. Afterwards, she cried with resolve: "It is good! It is good! It is good!" She pointed to her heart, grinning. "I have peace."

Yet to all who received him, to those who believed in his name, he gave the right to become children of God.

JOHN 1:12 NIV

"The angels are having a party in heaven right now because you are one of God's children," my

225

husband encouraged her.

"Great! Great! Great!" she replied with childlike belief.

We continued to visit Dana in the hospital. Her tumors grew back and doubled in size. But she remembered her experience. Though riddled with pain, she managed a glowing smile each visit. When we left on vacation, our pastor continued to visit Dana.

Two days after we returned, God called Dana home. The family asked my husband to conduct the funeral. It was a victorious celebration and message of hope.

We learned later that her husband prayed to receive Jesus the same night as Dana. We're still praying for the family. And my friendship with Lana has continued.

Those who sow in tears will reap with songs of joy.

PSALM 126:5 NIV

As my husband and I gathered around the family to plan the funeral after Dana's death, Lana approached us and hugged us warmly. She had shown little emotion until now. "I really appreciate you both. You have really made a difference in our lives," she said tearfully.

"Thank you, Jesus," I whispered. "It was You who made the difference."

⟿

Jesus went inside again and walked back into the kitchen of my home. Memories flooded my mind. Had the walls of my heart shrunk in such a short time? Years had passed since Dana had died. I had been asking God to increase my influence and allow me to share His love with others. But at times it seemed my heart had cooled and turned inward. And life had filled up with things—good things that crowded out the best. Would His heart ever feel at home here?

"Can you still bake pies?" Jesus asked. I nodded and understood. Like the man throwing back the starfish into the ocean, I, too, could make a difference—one pie at a time, one life at a time.

Devote yourself to "doing smaller things. . .with greater faithfulness,"[x] says Donna Partow. Whether one pie, one smile, one story, one visit, one child, one life—Jesus will expand our influence by pulling back the earthly walls of our hearts and allowing us, like Dana, to see a glimpse of heaven.

Jesus had kept His promise. When the last tear had dried on the disciples' faces, they remembered His words to them, " 'In my Father's house are many rooms; if it were not so, I would have told you. I am going there to prepare a place for you. And if I go and prepare a place for you, I will come back and take you to be with me that you also may be where I am' " (John 14:2–3 NIV). He had spent all this time helping me prepare a place for His presence here in my heart. Now He was allowing me the privilege all of His children have: to prepare a place in our hearts for others—and to let them know how to make Jesus feel at home in their hearts, too.

I stepped back and looked at Jesus' renovations. Together, we did a final walk-through. At the end of His inspection, my Master Designer smiled and said, "It is good." I knew it was just the beginning of a renewed relationship. With grateful tears in my eyes, I knelt at His feet again. At that moment, I remembered a dying mother's words to her evangelist son, Michael Gott: "You may never be the world's most famous evangelist. But you *can* be the most grateful." I felt the same way.

Then Jesus, knowing my thoughts, said, "What is it, child? There's something troubling you."

"What if. . .how long will it last. . .how can I keep. . ." Somehow the words hung in my throat. I needed His assurance one more time.

"If you will let me, I will always be at work renovating your heart. That's *my* part—to make it beautiful. All I ask. . . all I want. . .is your obedience and love."

I smiled in agreement as Jesus stooped and gently took my hand, lifting me to my feet again. I was already visualizing new kitchen curtains and a bigger back porch.

Master Designer Secret

Love never fails.

1 CORINTHIANS 13:8 NIV

Heart Check

Who needs your love—and His—today?

Loving Touches

No Fail Apple Pie

FILLING	CRUST
1 can pie-sliced apples	2 cups flour
$\frac{2}{3}$ cup sugar	$\frac{1}{2}$ cup vegetable oil
$\frac{1}{3}$ cup honey (or less)	$\frac{1}{2}$ cup skim milk
2 tsp. cinnamon	$\frac{1}{2}$ tsp. salt
$\frac{1}{2}$ tsp. nutmeg	$\frac{1}{2}$ tsp. cinnamon
1 Tbsp. lemon juice	(optional)
2–3 Tbsp. flour	

Preheat oven to 400 degrees. Add salt and flour; pour milk into vegetable oil and add to flour mixture. Gently stir and form dough into two equal balls. Put one ball between two pieces of waxed paper. Roll out dough to size of pie pan. Then carefully lift off top layer of waxed paper. Turn dough over and lay in pie pan. Gently peel off bottom layer of waxed paper and finish forming piecrust to fit the pan. Add all ingredients for filling. Pour into piecrust. Repeat procedure for top crust and carefully place on top of filling, peeling off top layer of waxed paper. Bake for 20 minutes. Reduce heat to 375 degrees for 20 to 25 minutes, or until crust is golden brown. Serve with a large scoop of vanilla ice cream and a generous portion of love.

[I] Henry Rische, "The Windows of Heaven," *The Encyclopedia of Religious Quotations,* edited and compiled by Frank S. Mead (New Jersey: Fleming H. Revell Company, 1965), p. 231.

[II] *The Encyclopedia of Religious Quotations,* edited and compiled by Frank S. Mead (New Jersey: Fleming H. Revell Company, 1965), p. 144.

[III] *The Family Circle Book,* edited by Erika Douglas (New York: Times Books, 1982), p. 172.

[IV] Sherwood Wirt, *Getting Into Print* (Nashville: Thomas Nelson, 1977), pp. 109–110.

[V] E.C. McKenzie, *14,000 Quips and Quotes* (Massachusetts: Hendrickson Publishers, Inc., 2000), p. 293.

[VI] Rebecca Barlow Jordan, *Courage for the Chicken Hearted, Humorous & Inspiring Stories for Confident Living,* by Becky Freeman, Susan Duke, Rebecca Barlow Jordan, Gracie Malone, & Fran Caffey Sandin (Tulsa, OK: Honor Books, 1998), p. 12.

[VII] Robert Fulghum, *All I Really Need to Know I Learned in Kindergarten* (New York: Ballantine Books, 1986, 1988), pp. 4–5.

[VIII] Max Lacado, *In the Grip of Grace* (Dallas, TX: Word Publishing, 1996), p. 123.

[IX] Richard A. Swenson, M.D., *Margin, How to Create the Emotional, Physical, Financial, & Time Reserves You Need* (Colorado Springs, CO: NavPress, 1992), p. 155.

[X] Donna Partow, *Walking in Total God-Confidence* (Minneapolis, MN: Bethany House Publishers, 1999), p. 180.

THE AUTHOR

Rebecca Barlow Jordan is the best-selling coauthor of *Courage for the Chicken Hearted* and *Eggstra Courage for the Chicken Hearted* (Honor Books). Her inspirational words also appear in seven other books, including *Seasons of a Woman's Heart* and *Treasures of a Woman's Heart* (Starburst), as well as over 1,600 greeting cards, articles, poems, devotionals, and gift products. She speaks at women's conferences, churches, and retreats and lives in Greenville, Texas, with her minister husband, Larry. Rebecca's family includes two married daughters and sons-in-law.

—❧

If this book has encouraged you in any way, I'd love to hear from you.

Rebecca is also available for speaking engagements. You may contact her at:

P. O. Box 8323
Greenville, TX 75404–8323

or by contacting

Speak Up Speaker Services
Toll free at (888) 870-7719 or at the following E-mail address:
Speakupinc@aol.com

For more information, see Rebecca's Web site at:
www.rebeccabarlowjordan.com